The Book of Revelation

Alfred Heidenreich

The Book
of
Revelation

Floris Books

First published in 1977 by Floris Books

This edition published in 2009

© 1977 The Christian Community
All right reserved. No part of this publication may
be reproduced without the prior permission of
Floris Books, 15 Harrison Gardens, Edinburgh.
www.florisbooks.co.uk

British Library CIP Data available

ISBN 978-086315-699-1

Printed in Great Britain
by Cpod, Trowbridge

Contents

Acknowledgements

Acknowledgement is due to Rudolf Steiner Press, London, for the quotations (in lecture 4, 5 and 7) from its translation of Rudolf Steiner's *The Apocalypse of St. John.*

Preface

Of all the titles that a publisher could consider for republication, this is perhaps the least likely to have lost its relevance after forty years. It has timeless quality – in part at least because its subject matter is time itself, in its greatest cycles.

The Book of Revelation places the reader, in whatever time they may be living, into a context where history and future over-arch the development of humanity, providing a context and frame of reference for the events of the particular moment.

When these lectures were held, the Cold War, Vietnam and student unrest were dominating the headlines. News of equal portent is there today as this republication appears – a valuable reminder of the perspective that we need to have at all times, whether they be stormy or peaceful.

The lectures were held in Rudolf Steiner House, London, in 1968, one year before Alfred Heidenreich's sudden death while on a visit to South Africa. As in the previous year, when he had spoken on the Gospels, the lecture hall was full. There was a great interest in the subject matter; there was as well a lively appreciation for his warm and knowledgeable presentations, which were accessible to old friends and newcomers alike. Over a period of forty years – since he and Martha Heimeran came as priests to England – he had been a central contributor to the work of renewing religious under-standing and practice out of the background of Anthro-posophy on these shores.

Included in this volume are some of the questions and answers which followed the lectures as well as a rendering of the text of the Book of Revelation by Alfred Heidenreich. This was intended by him not as an exact translation but as an aid to deepening appreciation of the content of this remarkable book.

Malcolm Allsop

The Imagery and Composition of the Book of Revelation

The Apocalypse* or, to give the book the name it has in the Roman Catholic New Testament, *The Secret Revelation of the Blessed Apostle John*, or, as it is called in the Authorized Version, *The Revelation of St. John the Divine*, is, as everybody knows, the last book of the New Testament. It poses a very serious question concerning the human mind: it raises the question of the human consciousness, and throws down a challenge to it.

The Germans have a proverb which says: 'If there is a hollow sound when a book and a head bump together, it does not necessarily mean that the hollow sound comes from the book.' And if we find it almost impossible to make head or tail of the Book of Revelation at a first reading, or perhaps even at a seventh reading, it is not necessarily the fault of the book. It simply means that we have very radically to change the wavelengths of our mind; we have to transform the very pattern, the very type of our ordinary consciousness.

This idea of a change of consciousness is today no longer quite so startling or unusual as it was even not so very long ago, when Rudolf Steiner's fundamental teaching of a path of development of the human

* The word is Greek and literally means something like *uncovering*.

13

consciousness was a path taught and followed in comparative isolation from the general public. This is no longer the case to the same extent; an increasing number of people begin to feel that something *can* be done, and something *ought* to be done, about a possible extension of the range and the depth of our consciousness. In a way, the intellect has had its run, and we feel we stand at a threshold of new things. It is perhaps still true that the majority of rationalists and humanists are rather cagey about this, and the general popular scientific mentality still shrinks back from it; but by way of introduction to our great subject, it is interesting and worthwhile to remember that throughout the scientific age, from the Renaissance to our own day, not only seers like William Blake* took an interest in these matters, but the very greatest scientists themselves.

I should like to call to witness the three greatest scientists of the British scientific age – three princes of science: Francis Bacon, Isaac Newton and Charles Darwin. Bacon, who is very aptly called the Father of Modern Science, wrote partly still in Latin, and I quote a sentence in which he refers to the need for the human soul to adapt itself and to expand to embrace the mysteries of the world.

Animus ad amplitudinem Mysteriorum pro modolo suo dilatetur: non Mysteria ad angustias animi constringantur.

'The soul can be expanded, in its own way, to the vastness of the mysteries, but the mysteries cannot be constrained, constricted, to the narrowness of the human soul.' A profound motto for any honest

* Mentioned in the chairman's introduction.

14

thinker, and particularly a profound motto and guiding thought for anybody who wishes to approach the Book of Revelation.

When the tercentenary of Newton's birth was celebrated in 1943, his Bible, which had been in private hands, was handed over as a gift to his college in Cambridge, Trinity College, and of course it was studied with interest by the college authorities. They found there were two books in that Bible which were thoroughly used and thumbed: the Book of Daniel in the Old Testament, the Book of Revelation in the New Testament. It was interesting to discover that the man to whom we owe, as it were, the final rounding off of the modern world conception initiated by Kepler and Copernicus, and the laying of the foundation of the mechanical world view with which we have been living since that time, had that urge, as his Bible bears out, to move in the field of vision, in the field of revelation, as a kind of counter-balance to the one-sided vision or intellectual concept of a mechanised and mechanical universe.

And the third one, perhaps most surprisingly, is Charles Darwin. It is perhaps not generally known that before he published his book, *The Origin of Species*, he wondered whether he should call it *The Development of Species*, which some people think might have been a more adequate title. But, partly in order to throw down the gauntlet to the theologians, he finally called it *The Origin of Species*. There are, however, certain passages in it where the old idea of describing the *development*, rather than the origin, of species (rather as in our day Teilhard de Chardin does), breaks through. This is particularly evident in the

15

chapter where he speaks of the development of the eye, the principal sense organ. In the same way that one can say that the chapter about the origin of language is the most pathetic chapter in *The Origin of Species*, the chapter on the development of the eye is the most moving. Speaking of that he says:

> We must suppose that there is a power represented by natural selection,

(not natural selection itself)

> or the survival of the fittest, always intently watching each slight alteration, and carefully preserving each which tends to produce a distincter image.

A power watching this development . . . And then comes the sentence that has a bearing on what we are discussing as an introduction:

> May we not believe that a living optical instrument might thus be formed as superior to one of glass, as the works of the Creator are to those of man?

So writes Charles Darwin in *The Origin of Species*.

And there you have the witness of these three princes of science to the possibility and the *need* to transcend the normal, narrow, restricted type of consciousness which we use to run our daily lives; we can go beyond it. And now, in order to come to grips with the Apocalypse, we *need* that vision of Bacon which believes in the dilation of the human soul to comprehend the mysteries; we *need* that personal and passionate activity of Newton to read the Book of Daniel and the Book of Revelation to balance the mechanical world-picture; we *need* the belief of Darwin that a *living* eye, a living optical instrument, can be created in man which is as superior to one of glass as the works of the Creator are to those of man.

*   *   *

It is now with these ideas, these critical and practical considerations in mind that we approach the book. Instead of reading straight away from it, let me remind you, perhaps, of some of the more general impressions which the one or the other of you might have had, and which might come representatively to expression in the work of an American and of a British writer. The American, A. C. Benson, writes about his impression in a more joyful mood than the other. His book is actually called *Joyous God*, from which I have quoted already in my translator's note to the book on the Apocalypse by my late friend, Emil Bock.* He writes as follows, giving a first general impression:

> I think of it as an awful and spontaneous energy of spiritual life going on, of which the prophet was enabled to catch a glimpse. Those 'voices crying day and night', 'the new song that was before the throne', the cry of 'come and see' – these are but part of a vast and urgent business, which the prophet was allowed to overhear. It is not a silent place, that highest heaven, of indolence and placid peace, but a scene of fierce activity, and the clamour of mighty voices.

And this is what Francis Thompson writes, rather more gloomily, about his general impression of the Apocalypse:

> ... I was greatly, though vaguely, impressed by the mysterious imagery, the cloudy grandeurs of the *Apocalypse*. Deeply uncomprehended, it was, of course, the pageantry of an

* *The Apocalypse of St. John*, Emil Bock, The Christian Community Press, London, 1957.

appalling dream: insurgent darkness, with wild lights flashing through it; terrible phantasms, insupportably revealed against profound light, and in a moment no more; on the earth, hurryings to and fro, like insects of the hearth at a sudden candle; unknown voices uttering out of darkness darkened and disastrous speech; and all this in motion and turmoil like the sands of a fretted pool.*

*   *   *

But now, approaching more directly, we ought to proceed, as it is always wise in these matters, from the known to the unknown; and that means that we should, however briefly, acknowledge the intense work of academic theological scholarship that has gone into the analysis and study of this great book. There are mainly two schools we have to mention. The one is the school of the ordinary textual and literary criticism. One can only admire the beehive industry of the theological scholars which has examined every single word, analysed the whole book, and been mainly concerned to find that this particular image can be traced here, and that particular vision there, giving the kind of pedigree of the various images and ideas in the usual manner of the literary historian. And yet this does not help one greatly; it does not really *explain* much. It does not tell you much about Shakespeare if you just know from where the one or the other of his subject matters was taken; it tells you nothing about the genius of Shakespeare or the wonderful texture of his plays. So it is with the Apocalypse, and we shall not take much notice of the results of that type of research.

* 'Books that have influenced me', *Weekly Register*, 26 January, 1900.

Then there is the other school which relates the Apocalypse to contemporary events. It is generally held that the Apocalypse reflects either the persecution under Nero or the persecution under Domitian at the end of the first century; that in some of its visions of the Throne there is a reflection of the ceremony and protocol of the imperial court in Rome, and things of that kind, which are quite interesting, and to which at one time or another in the course of our lectures we shall have occasion to refer.

But now let us concentrate on a problem in which our own interest on the very first evening and the interest of academic scholarship coincide, and that is the question of authorship. Who wrote the Book of Revelation? Who is this Blessed Apostle John, this St. John the Divine? General theological scholarship has come to the conclusion that the book indeed shows the kind of general spirit and atmosphere of what is known as the Johannine presentation of Christianity, but it has also come to the conclusion that it is impossible to assume that the Apostle John *wrote* it. The reason for this is that the Apostle John, if we take him to be the son of Zebedee and brother of James, died a martyr's death in the year 56 in Jerusalem, and, for a number of reasons arising from both internal and external evidence, the Apocalypse cannot have been written before 70, and very likely was not written before A.D. 95, which would be forty years after the death of John, the son of Zebedee. The answer to that riddle can be given from the research of Rudolf Steiner, which he has extended to the personality, character and development of the mysterious figure called John.

19

In his very first book dealing with Christian matters, published in 1902 under the title, *Christianity As Mystical Fact*, Rudolf Steiner devotes a whole chapter to the incident recorded in St. John's Gospel and generally known as the Raising of Lazarus. In the series of lectures on the New Testament* I gave here a year ago, I devoted an evening to this, and obviously cannot go over the whole matter again. But the principle of it is that Rudolf Steiner describes this whole incident as a veiled initiation of Lazarus, who went through the kind of death the neophyte underwent in the ancient mysteries, although in a rather special way, and then was raised back to life. The event is covered and camouflaged in the way usual in ancient days, because it was forbidden, under pain of death, to speak directly and openly about these mysteries. Rudolf Steiner then leads on to the conclusion that this Lazarus is the author of the Fourth Gospel. If those to whom this idea is new wish to pursue it further, I can only recommend reading the book by Steiner I have mentioned. You will find it remarkably convincing, even at the first reading. It answers a number of questions which the text of the eleventh chapter of St. John's Gospel presents to the attentive reader.

If we accept this, then of course the whole problem of authorship appears in a different light. Then we deal with another personality; then it is perfectly possible to accept what a considerable number of early Christian authorities do accept, that the author is the elder John, the presbyter John, who lived in Ephesus at the end of the first century. Of him the story is told

* Now published under the title *The Unknown in the Gospels*, The Christian Community Press, London, 1972.

that when he was nearly one hundred years old, he attended the Communion service, the Eucharist, and at the end got up and simply said: 'Children, love one another.' And the story goes that his moral presence was so tremendous that fountains of love flowed from him and inspired the people. The tradition that he was the John of whom we speak goes back, even with documentary evidence, to the middle of the second century, to Justin, Irenaeus, Clement of Alexandria, Tertullian and the so-called Canon of Muratori, all second- and early third-century writers.

Even if we accept that, however, there is still one great problem to which the scholars point. The style, the choice of words, the manner of expression of the Apocalypse, is so very different both from the Gospel and from the Epistles of St. John. It is written in a most extraordinary language. The words are Greek, but, broadly speaking, the grammar is Hebrew. It is like the language of a German refugee speaking good English, but thinking in German, translating into what passes as English but really has German grammar and German idiom. Some such quality can be traced in the style of writing in the Book of Revelation. But is it *only* because John thought in Hebrew and wrote in Greek? It is not very likely if we consider this the last of his writings.

Now here I venture an explanation for which I have nobody else's authority, and you must take it for what it is worth on my own suggestion. In Rudolf Steiner's basic – I might almost call it – textbook for the development of higher forces and powers of knowledge and vision, *Knowledge of the Higher Worlds. How is it achieved?*, there is a chapter in which he describes what happens to the human soul at a certain stage of its pilgrimage on the esoteric path. It is something that happens involuntarily today in a chaotic and sometimes pathological manner to a number of people: a kind of disengagement between the natural co-ordination of thinking, feeling and willing takes place. We all know the person who can think the most brilliant ideas, yet can never carry them out because there is no co-ordination between the thoughts in the head and the will-forces that would bring these thoughts into action. Or the opposite: 'the bull in the china shop' who rushes ahead, with no rational light illuminating his tempestuous action. Or the person carried away by his emotions. This is a kind of a caricature, or, as Dostoevsky would have said, a *monkey* reflection of the real thing. And the real thing is that at a certain stage of the development of the soul towards its unfolding of higher powers, these three faculties of the soul – thinking, feeling and willing – assume a relative independence, and have to be co-ordinated voluntarily, arbitrarily, as a matter of self-discipline.

If we assume that this John, who had passed through an initiation, had his soul faculties differentiated in this way, an entirely new light falls on the relative differences of literary style, and also of content, when we compare the Gospel, the Epistles and the Book of Revelation. In the Gospel we have inspired thought; the Gospel of St. John is sublime thought, the most wonderful level of pure Christian thought. In the Epistles we have the essence of feeling; take particularly the fourth chapter of the First Epistle and its wonderful description of Christian love, culminating in that simple sentence: *God is love; and he that dwelleth in love dwelleth in God, and God in him.* The whole Epistle consists of variations on this great subject. John is there writing in the sphere of his heart. And when he comes to the Book of Revelation, he writes in the sphere of his will.

If you analyse the quality of the ancient languages, Latin, Greek and Hebrew, you find in Latin a highly intellectual language, a language of definitions (we use Latin phrases in legal language right to this day). Greek is the language of beauty; it comes more from the heart. Even if you think of the philosophical writings of Plato and Aristotle, their attraction lies in the fact that they are not just intellectual thought, but artistic thought. Hebrew is the language of the will, in its whole structure, grammar and sound; the very fact that no vowels but only consonants are written in it gives you an idea of the nature of that language. We can take the theory, for what it is worth (it is as good as any other, I think, that has been advanced on the subject) that the remarkable style of the Book of Revelation is a combination of the will-forces of the Hebrew background with the kind of expression that the Greek of the time allowed. It is a somewhat primitive Greek. C. S. Lewis called it 'basic Greek'. Like 'basic English', it does not use a great many words, but it has a terse beauty of its own. And practically all the scholars, although in a way they tear it to pieces and show what bad grammar it has, finally come to express their appreciation of that particular simplicity which *speaks* to you, and speaks to you as the language of the will. If we take these ideas into consideration, we can see the variety in the unity; there is the one author, but at one time speaking from

23

his thinking head, another time from his feeling heart, and, in the Apocalypse, from his devoted will.

This connection with the will also comes to expression in the structure of the book. It is in the structure, the logical sequence of a book, or even an essay, where the will expresses itself. If you want to get something done, you have so to order your thoughts that they *lead* to something. The Book of Revelation is a most wonderful unit, and I have often wondered how those who pull it to pieces and think it has been collected from here there and everywhere can explain its absolute unity of style, of language and of structure. It moves (and in one of the later lectures I will explain why) in great stages of seven: seven letters to the seven churches in Asia, followed by the seven seals, followed by the seven trumpets, followed by the seven vials of wrath. And this fourfold sevenhood is introduced by the vision of the Son of Man, the great vision of archetypal Man, and is concluded by the picture of the New Jerusalem, the human community, the City. You are led from Man to the human Community in these great four-times-seven stages. There you have the *structure*.

The sequence of these four sevenhoods again reveals a deeper order of things. They are not just a literary device. Here again I must refer to some of the fundamental books of Rudolf Steiner on the development of the human soul, the esoteric path. As many of you who have been readers of Steiner for some time will well know, he describes the development of higher knowledge in three stages. The first stage he describes as Imagination. This is more than ordinary phantasy; it is a kind of living in pictures, pictures which press into the soul and yet are created by the co-operation of the soul. He explains how in order to understand them fully the mind must operate with such concentration that it can remove these pictures, and then, into the quiet and empty mind, Inspiration comes, voices speak and explain what the pictures wish to reveal. The third stage he calls Intuition, in its highest and technical sense: a meeting face to face with spiritual beings. Now, if we take these three stages of higher knowledge which Steiner describes from many angles time and again because they are essential, we have the key to the plan of the Book of Revelation.

We leave aside for the moment the opening vision of Man and the closing vision of the City, and begin with the seven letters, the seven messages to the seven churches. There we find ourselves, so to speak, still in the world of normal consciousness where letters can be written, although they are inspired letters — they are sent by an angel. Then come the seven seals. The book describes that there is a scroll sealed with seven seals, and then the imagery begins to be puzzling because, in order to read a scroll or to open it, you would have thought you had to open all the seven seals. But no: the moment the first seal is opened an imagination appears: a white horse; on the opening of the second seal, a red horse; the third seal, a black horse; the fourth seal, a pallid horse. It is as if the seals are buds, flowers, which open up. The first four seals are opened in quick succession, and these pictures appear. The fifth seal is extended; and then comes, characteristically: 'And when he opened the seventh seal there was silence in heaven for half an hour.' You reach a kind of interval. This is precisely what Rudolf Steiner describes as happening when you pass on the path of higher knowledge from Imagination to Inspiration. It is what he calls the stage of empty consciousness. Complete silence for half an hour (whatever that may be) but there, qualitatively, is that interval. And what comes now?

'And I saw the seven angels which stood before God, and to them were given seven trumpets.' Now follows Inspiration in seven trumpet calls. When that is concluded comes what is translated as 'the Vials of Wrath'. That is how the reformers thought about it, but what they translated as *wrath* is really *fierce love*, fierce consuming love. How can the fierce consuming love of the spiritual beings become wrath? Rudolf Steiner gave a very homely explanation: he said you could imagine a clear stream of water coming from above, but then passing through a dirty sponge so that what comes out on the other side is not clear, but looks dirty; and it takes quite a time until the sponge has cleared. In this way he tried to explain how the fierce stream of divine love entering into humanity cannot *directly* enter because there is the dirty sponge which humanity in a way produces, and which has first to be pierced. So for the time being very often the divine love appears as divine wrath. What we may often experience in our life as a tragedy, as a chastisement of God, a punishment, as people say, is a manifestation of divine love, but within the setting of human realities and facts *appearing* as a manifestation of wrath, of anger. Once these last seven (shall I say?) 'vessels of consuming love' pass, then it is the time, the stage is set, for the New Jerusalem to be built.

*　　*　　*

26

Now let us look at the opening verses. I read first from the well-known Authorised Version.

> The revelation of Jesus Christ, which God gave unto him, to show unto his servants things which must shortly come to pass; and he sent and signified it unto his servant John: Who bare record of the word of God, and of the testimony of Jesus Christ, and of all things that he saw. Blessed is he that readeth, and they that hear the words of this prophecy, and keep those things which are written therein: for the time is at hand.

I believe even if one does not understand it, and is quite outside this whole range of experience, it makes a strange appeal. And now allow me to read it in my own translation, which perhaps brings out one or two details a little more closely. Where we read 'God', at least in the first sentence, I have added the phrase used in the liturgy of The Christian Community: *the Ground of the World*, simply because 'God' is a word which really no longer strikes one; it is devalued.

> This is the revelation of Jesus Christ which God, the Ground of the World, has given him, in order to show those who serve him what is to come, and what is approaching at a quickening pace. He has set it out in pictures . . .

signified says the old translation; the Greek word used is the one which we use in the word *semantics* –

> . . . and sent it through his angel to his servant John, who gave witness to the Word who had come from God, and to the living testimony of Jesus Christ, all of which he saw with his own eyes. Blessed is he who reads the words of this prophecy; and those who listen and ponder the things which are written in it; for this is the time.

I want to draw your attention to the veritable

Jacob's ladder of descent from God to man which you find in this introduction. Immediately there appears a kind of deliberate, wilful structure. We read of the revelation of Jesus Christ which *God, the Ground of the World*, has given to *Him*. He has set it in pictures and sent it through *His angel* to *His servant, John* – man. (And John is qualified in a twofold way, that he gave testimony to the Word of God – that links it with the Gospel – and to the divine testimony of Jesus, all of which he saw with his own eyes – which refers to Golgotha.) Blessed is *he who reads* (singular) and *those who listen* and *who ponder what is written*. It is generally understood, and I think rightly, that these early Christian books, or letters, were read in a group, and therefore there is the singular, *he who reads*, and the plural, *those who listen and ponder*. And so you have this wonderful descent described at the beginning: from God, to Christ, to His angel, to John, to the reader and to the listeners.

And then this first section ends with: 'For *ò kairos eggys.*' This is extremely difficult to translate. It gives the idea that the time is *pressing*. 'For this is the *time.*' It is a phrase which one can say refers to a particular moment in history, but it is a kind of signature tune which goes through the whole Apocalypse. *This is the time.* And, as we shall see when we go on to study the book further, it depends to some extent on the *reader* whether he makes it his time or not. It is not just that 1968 is the time either; it might be any time. But this is the time: the moment when you make contact with the world revealed in the Apocalypse.

I will just read now from my own translation a few more verses, to give the impression of the *solemnity* of

28

the opening, the kind of liturgical character the book has.

> John to the seven churches in Asia: grace and peace be to you from him who is, who was, and who is to come . . .

That phrase comes several times and is a transformation of the old Hebrew phrase, 'I AM the I AM'. The presence of the 'I AM' is now unfolded as He who was, who is, and who is to come.

> . . . and from the seven Creator-Spirits before his throne (that is the Elohim), and from Jesus Christ the faithful witness, the first-born from the realm of the dead, the principal of all the rulers of the earth. To him who loves us, who through the power of his blood frees us from the sickness of sin, who has made us into a kingdom, and priests for God his father, to him be glory and power through all cycles of time. Amen.

Then comes the other subject with which the Apocalypse deals: all the events which are described are set in motion through a new pressure of Christ on humanity, a new presence, a new *parousia*.

> See, he comes in the realm of the clouds. Every eye shall see him, even those who pierced him. Men of every kind on the earth shall be shaken to their depths because of him. Yea, so be it. I am the Alpha and the Omega, says the lord, who is, who was, who will be, who rules the universe.

Perhaps one could translate this last clause better (it contains the Greek word *pantocrator* 'who rules everything, who has power over everything'. It is the apocalyptic translation of the earlier Hebrew, *Jahve Sabaoth*, the Lord of Hosts. We find in the Apocalypse a kind of transformation of some of the liturgical phrases of the Old Testament concentrated on Christ;

29

and one of the subjects we have to study as we go along is this transformation of some of the visions of the Old Testament, the visions of Jahve, in whom the sublime deity was reflected, now transferred to and transformed into the qualities of Christ.

*　　*　　*

Now, just one last thought in this introductory lecture. We can read the Book of Revelation in the way we have just begun, and perhaps already we have felt that the mere reading as literature will not be quite satisfactory. I have in the past, on several occasions, read the whole book in one session to a small group of people. One does not understand everything – that is impossible – but it has an almost uncanny effect. Later on in the book, the angel who brings the little book says that it should not only be read, but eaten. 'Take it, and eat it up; and it shall make thy belly bitter but it shall be in thy mouth sweet as honey.' The Book of Revelation itself is a book which at first taste is interesting and perhaps even sweet; but if you let it pass into yourself, a transformation begins: it is uncomfortable, it is indigestible, your stomach does not like it. But the positive side of this is that you get involved. It is most emphatically a book which, as you go along, you can no longer read with the ordinary onlooker-consciousness with which we live in the world. We look at everything from outside, and very rarely become deeply moved. That is really impossible with this book. It may happen that after a while you throw it into the corner; that is one way of dealing with it. But, if you do not do that, your onlooker-consciousness is undermined, it is destroyed. It is one of the interesting things about this book, compared for instance with the prophetic books of the Old Testament, that John, the writer, is constantly *actively* involved. He is moved into the spirit; but then he is bidden, 'Come and see', and he is asked questions: 'Who is this?' and answers: 'Sir, you know.' He is constantly involved, until he is taken by the angel on to the mountain and sees the New Jerusalem. He is an *actor* in it, not just there as a passive receiver of a revelation. He is actively involved in the whole process of which the book speaks.

That is the character the book has and can communicate to us. It will ultimately make sense only if we feel we want to be actors, actors in that great cosmic drama, that we want to be involved in this development – from having a vision of archetypal man to the creation of the New Jerusalem. I hope it will be on these lines that we can continue.

There were some people in the early church, more particularly in the eastern part, who had doubts whether this book was to be included in the New Testament canon. It is very characteristic that it was mainly the western fathers, whom I mentioned earlier, who accepted it and put it into the canon of sacred scripture. Perhaps it was a bit too uncanny for the eastern members of the church; and in particular, there was, of course, a good deal of apocalyptical literature in the eastern countries of an apocryphal type, and perhaps they overlooked the fact that this book is called the revelation of *Jesus Christ*. It is not a revelation only *about* Him, or primarily about Him, but *of* Him, *by* Him. It is the content of the consciousness of Christ after His resurrection, one might say; and it is on to that level that we are lifted, into that development, into that process, that we are invited to enter, not as readers only, not as listeners, not as onlookers, but as *actors*.

Questions and answers were recorded after this lecture. See p. 151

The Son of Man – The Seven Churches –
What the Spirit Says to the Churches

Last time we endeavoured to get a general picture of
that great book which is composed like a musical
symphony, with its prelude and postlude and four
great movements. After this we had a closer look at the
first half of the opening chapter, and saw how the first
verses lead like a Jacob's ladder from heaven to earth:
from God to Christ, from Christ to His angel, from
His angel to John, from John to the reader, from the
reader to the hearers, from the hearers to those who
ponder the message. Seven distinct stages lead from
the spiritual world to the earth.

Today, we go further in the first, second and third
chapters, discuss in more detail the opening vision and
then the messages, the epistles to the seven churches in
Asia. We will resume the text half way through the
first chapter. I will read this particular passage in my
own translation, not very different, but in one or two
details perhaps rather more direct than the somewhat
archaic Authorised Version.

I, John, your brother, who shares the trials and the kingship
and the patient expectation . . .

these are the three apocalyptic virtues or experiences –

. . . to which Jesus calls us, found myself on the island of
Patmos, because I had preached the word of God and had

witnessed for Jesus. And there on the Lord's day the spiritual world was opened to me and I heard from behind me a powerful voice like a trumpet call . . .

'I John': here the writer mentions his name in this simple form. He does the same in the last chapter. Even in this respect, the composition of the book is quite deliberate. The New English Bible translates, 'I am John'. You may do so. But, you remember, this John is Lazarus who had gone through what is described as a death and been raised back to life again – a story which, however, is a kind of cover story disguising an initiation. In this initiation he became overshadowed by the spirit of John the Baptist, and henceforth is known as John, and is the author of the Gospel, the Epistles of John and the Book of Revelation. I also tried to explain why the literary style of the Book of Revelation is so very different from that of the Gospel and causes literary critics among modern scholars to think it is impossible the same man wrote both books, although early Christian tradition, right from about the year 150 forward, maintains the identity of the author of the Fourth Gospel with the author of the Johannine Epistles and the author of the Book of Revelation.

John was in Patmos and it is assumed that he was sent there during the persecution under Domitian in 95, and that the order for his relegation was probably issued by the Governor of Asia Minor, not necessarily by the Emperor himself. At this point, the Authorised Version says, 'I was in the spirit'. The New English Bible and the Jerusalem Bible say, 'I was possessed by the spirit' – which I think is certainly worse than 'I was in the Spirit'. It is something of a concession to modern ideas that if you are 'in the spirit' you must be *possessed* by the spirit. This, I think, is quite misleading. John's writing is inspired, but not dictated. He was not *possessed* as a medium. I think it would be still more adequate, perhaps in line with the language we are gradually developing on the basis of Rudolf Steiner's teaching, and equally true to say, 'The spiritual world was opened to me'.

This may for a moment give one pause as an ordinary person wondering whether such things are really possible; but then one can reflect that while perhaps till thirty years ago, let alone fifty years ago, these matters were very much more doubted and questioned by people, today spiritual experience (or as it is known now, 'extra-sensory perception'), is accepted more universally as a fact of life. But, we should appreciate from the beginning that this kind of spiritual experience which is revealed to us in the Book of Revelation is one of especial depths and especial grandeur. Perhaps we may take a lead from a charming little book which a friend brought back to me from Patmos; you acquire one when you visit the grotto in which John is supposed to have lived and composed his Apocalypse. It is translated into a rather quaint English, but I read it as it stands.

The visitor must descend thirty steps in order to reach the saint portico through a yard full of flowers. This descent equals to a descent into our forgotten inner world. Especially today when man, having conquered space, has neglected completely his inner world. The descent brings us to the outer portico. A saint image of the Evangelist above the entrance, two marbled inscriptions, on each side of it and one above it, are its only adornment. The first inscription: 'As terrible this place . . .' brings us to Bethil where the staircase which united heaven and earth was constructed.

Bethel, you will remember, is what Jacob called the place where he had the vision of the ladder into heaven – Bethel, the Place of God. So this writer very rightly suggests that now we have met a second Bethel. And then he sums up this introduction which leads us, really, as he says, these thirty steps of descent into the inner world by saying:

> If in the Grotto of Bethlem the first whimperings of God's new-born son were heard, in the Grotto of Patmos were heard his last speeches.*

He takes the Book of Revelation as a kind of last legacy of Christ.

Before speaking on the Son of Man, I should like, if I may, to reverse the order, and say a word about the seven churches first. My reason for doing this is twofold. It is rather important that, when we set off on a spiritual journey which will lead us into very considerable heights, we should get an idea of the events and the people concerned being, all the same, firmly rooted in history. It is one of the most fundamental considerations about Christianity that it is an historical religion, that it is *rooted in history*, that it has an impact on history on every level of existence. To give just another parallel example, this, of course, is also why we mention Pontius Pilate in the Creed – saying that Christ 'was crucified under Pontius Pilate'. We do not mention this rather insignificant cavalry general, as he has been described, who got into prominence only

* Theodoritus Bournis, *The Unhewn Grotto of the Apocalypse*, Zissimos Virvillis, Athens, 1962.

36

because he was married to a princess of the imperial house, for his own significance, but as a way of dating, of indicating that *Golgotha happened in history* – not a mystical event, but, as Steiner says, a mystical *fact*, an event in history which had a mystical significance. And so I would like us to have the impression that at the beginning of the book we move, really, on the field of history, and rather an exciting field of history. By the same token, we follow our accepted method, as far as possible, of proceeding from the known to the unknown.

The ordinary reader will not, perhaps, agree that these places, these seven churches of Pergamum, Thyatira, even Ephesus, Laodicea etcetera, form something which is *known*, but that is really because most of these places are today part of Turkey, a country which, at any rate up until the last war, was not very frequently visited. The only place one knew much about was Smyrna, the modern Izmir, because it is the one still flourishing port on that coast of Asia Minor. As some of you may remember, it played an important part in a very tragic episode of modern history in the early twenties, when first the Greeks invaded it with a misguided idea of conquering their old land, and then the Turks under Kemal Pasha drove them out in 1922, at the same time driving about one and a half million Greeks from Asia Minor, who thereby really lost their last foothold in that part of the world. In addition to Smyrna, perhaps Ephesus has become a little more known because nowadays expeditions or excursions are led by motor coach from Izmir to Ephesus down the coast. And most recently of all have come conducted coach tours through the places of the seven churches in Asia. Whether that is owing to a reviving interest in this matter, or a sort of gimmick of travel agencies who want to offer ever new attractions and conquer new markets, I am not really quite sure, but you can do it. So, gradually perhaps, this forgotten world, these seven unknown old towns, some of them today nearly ruined places, are coming back into knowledge.

By contrast, towards the end of the first Christian century, at the time when the book is likely to have been written, this was the *centre*, the intellectual, cultural and spiritual centre, of the Roman Empire. This province, known as 'Asia Proconsularis', was the most cultured province of the whole Roman Empire. It was in a sense the eastern half of Greece. The western half was the part we know today: the peninsula with its islands, which in the first century had fallen into decadence. Athens had been eclipsed; Corinth had just survived as a commercial centre, not much of a cultural centre any more, in fact a commercial centre with an immoral reputation. But in the eastern half of Greece, Asia Minor, there the legacy of Greece was really preserved. It was a part of the universal Greek world, with a great tradition, a great surviving spiritual aura. It was the home of Homer, who is supposed to have been born in Smyrna; certainly the epics were born in that part of the world. It was also the home of Herodotus, the first great historian. It was the home of the early Greek philosopher, Thales, of Heraclitus and Pythagoras. They all came from that part of the world. In the first century it was that part of the Roman Empire where, on the one hand, the great religions of the east penetrated to the west and were received and amalgamated with Greek philosophy and with the birth of western thought, and, on the other, where they first came into contact with that kind of managerial consciousness which was born among the Romans. Rome, although it was the administrative centre of the great empire, was a barbarous city compared with this great centre of civilisation and culture, Asia Proconsularis.

In this setting, Ephesus, the first of the seven churches mentioned in the Book of Revelation, was the centre. It was the great port. Today it is no longer so because the river has silted up and the town is about three miles inland and has therefore lost its old splendour. It was the centre of the administration, having the office of the proconsul, or the governor, and was an immensely rich city with its magnificent set of temples, the greatest of which was the temple of Diana, of Artemis. Here, eastern fertility cults and western concepts of the spiritual significance of the feminine qualities in mankind flowed together, and it was a great centre of learning.

The seven churches, if I mention them now in the sequence in which they are given in the Book of Revelation, are situated along a kind of coach road. Remarkably enough they form a selection of seven out of twelve. There were twelve great Christian centres in about the year 100. Collossae is another one knows about from the Pauline letters; there was Hierapolis and Miletus.* The seven, however, are selected because they lie on a circular route going out from Ephesus and returning to it again. One can assume that this had been the circuit of John, the Presbyter of

* Magnesia and Tralles would complete the twelve in this area. *Ed.*

39

Ephesus, (call him a kind of bishop, perhaps, although the word was not yet used in the modern sense), who from time to time had visited these centres, and to whom he then wrote these messages. After Ephesus comes Smyrna, also a great port in those days, and then Pergamum. This was the private residence of the Governor and has the distinction of being the first place in which emperor-worship was introduced.* Then from Pergamum one goes on to Thyatira, less important, and to Sardes, which had once been the capital of the kingdom of Croesus. Then comes Philadelphia and finally Laodicea.

This is the circle of the seven churches, and although all seven, as we shall see presently, are treated in a different way on their respective merits, yet they are also treated on a basis of equality. From a structural, or if you like, social point of view, this is a very interesting phenomenon. The name for congregation and for church is identical: *ecclesia*. All seven are representatives of *the* ecclesia. This is interesting in view of some of the present-day ecumenical ideas and developments where there is, at any rate in certain circles, a strong tendency towards a unified, monolithic, streamlined church – 'una sancta ecclesia' – with one particular head and everything coming under the

---

* It is an interesting historical fact that emperor-worship did not start in Rome; it was introduced in Asia Minor, in Pergamum. As early as 29 B.C., Augustus (Octavianus as he then was) had a temple erected to him there, and it was there some years later that, for the first time, the emperor was officially proclaimed *Salvator orbis, invictus Dei filius* – 'The saviour of the world, the unconquered and unconquerable son of God'. All this grew in that remarkable soil, partly, of course, under the influence of oriental ideas: the great kings of Persia, the pharaohs of Egypt, always held this position of being worthy of divine worship and adoration.

jurisdiction of that head. This is distinctly *not* the conception of the Book of Revelation, or early Christianity as represented by the Book of Revelation. There is a variety of churches – seven are given as archetypes – with a unified spirit and a unified law as they would say, yet, as we shall see, quite *differentiated* in their particular backgrounds and their particular characters. This is a very important conception, because historically speaking the whole idea of an organisationally unified church is not a Christian idea at all. It is a Roman idea which came into the church through Constantine. If we really want to get to know living Christianity in its various aspects, we must go back before the year 300, before Constantine. From that point onward the church became Romanised. When we began to lay the foundations of The Christian Community, Rudolf Steiner always quite plainly advised us that if we wanted to get to know the real Christianity, and wanted to be guided and inspired by it, we must go back to the first three hundred years. I was most startled the other day to read in one of the papers that an Augustinian Catholic father (unfortunately his name was not given) said that the whole post-Constantinian history of the church could best be described in terms of the prodigal son while he was living by himself and wasting his substance with harlots and riotous living.

In the Book of Revelation and the description of the seven churches, we have a kind of vision, not a concept really, but a vision, of an organisation, a social pattern of Christianity, differentiated into seven equal forms of expression, seven equal archetypes. And now let us look at them.

Our last quotation ended with John's words, 'And there on the Lord's day the spiritual world was opened to me, and I heard from behind me a powerful voice . . .' That is a typical description of a spiritual experience which always seems to come, to start with, from behind – and then you have to turn round, you have to respond by making a movement.

> . . . I heard from behind me a powerful voice like a trumpet call, and it said, 'Write down what you see, and send it to the seven churches: to Ephesus, Smyrna, Pergamum, Thyatira, Sardes, Philadelphia, Laodicea'.

It would be beyond our possibilities now to analyse these seven messages in every detail, but we can make a few general remarks and then point out one or the other of the interesting differences. Each one has a certain style. In the first sentence of each message the being who instructs John to write reveals himself from a different angle. The seven revelations together make a wonderful description of the sevenfold manifestation of that being who speaks to John. Then follows in each case the statement, 'I know what you are doing'. It expresses the fact that there is a knowledge of the condition of a particular church. After that comes the actual message; in most cases a few encouraging things are said, and then a number of critical things – good psychology. Then comes a formula addressed to those who really win through; in the Greek the word *nike*, victory, is used. It is he who gains the victory, who wins through, to whom certain things shall be given, and these seven gifts are, again, differentiated. Each message closes with the formula, 'He who has ears to hear, let him hear what the Spirit says to the churches' — a formula obviously suggesting that just the ordinary, everyday, common or garden hearing is not quite good enough, that some deeper hearing is necessary. Of course, that increasingly applies to the whole Book of Revelation; I indicated that last time, and read it out again from the Patmos guide book: unless the human soul can be tuned into that level of spiritual manifestation, one not only will not understand it, but will find it meaningless and without significance.

Before describing the differences, I ought to mention one other factor: the letters are addressed not to the churches but the angel of each church. Ordinary scholarship says this was a way of naming the leader of the church, which up to a point is true, and Rudolf Steiner confirms this opinion. But the leader is, in a sense, the bearer of the higher spirit, the community spirit, the angel of the church. It is that comprehensive *consciousness* (a higher consciousness than that possessed by the individual), in a sense the spiritual *group-soul*, which is addressed. This, of course, is conscious of the virtues and feelings of a particular group and, as Rudolf Steiner explained once, is particularly conscious of the *mixture* in a particular church of what has come in as influence from eastern religion, as influence from Jewish tradition (because many of the original converts were Jews of the dispersion) and from other people who joined it. This mixture is typical of the early Christian churches; they were not homogenous people, by race, by social status, by ownership of property or wealth. It is quite wrong to think that they were all people on the social fringe, as it were; some of them were people of wealth and position. This kind of *conglomeration* of individuals, really taken out of their social groups and settings and brought together as an *ecclesia*, created a consciousness which lived there, and *that* was held in the soul of the angel of the church. It is to this soul of the angel that these messages are directed.

Now let us examine the seven manifestations of the being who inspires John. In the first letter he describes himself as the one who has the seven candlesticks and the seven stars. In the second one he describes himself as the first and the last, who was dead and is alive. In the third one he has the two-edged sword. In the fourth he has eyes like a flame of fire and feet of brass. Then in the fifth one again he has the seven stars, and the seven spirits of God. In the sixth he holds the key of David, and in the seventh one he describes himself as the Amen, the faithful and true witness.

The seven gifts promised to the victorious are also different: in the first message, those who are victorious are to be given to eat from the Tree of Life; in the second they are to be given the crown of life; in the third, they are promised the hidden manna and each a white stone with his name written on it; in the fourth one, a rod of iron breaking up the nations, and the morning star; in the fifth, white garments and their names not blotted from the book of life; in the sixth one, those who are victorious are to become pillars of the church; and in the seventh one, they are to be granted to sit with the spiritual figure on his throne.

So far this has been simply a summary, but in order to understand a little more deeply the significance of these seven tones of the scale, or seven colours of the rainbow, as expressed in the self-manifestation and the

44

gifts, I would like now, for a moment, to have a somewhat theoretical interlude and give a brief extract from what I would like to call almost a kind of catechism of an occult view of human evolution and history, in which the sevenhood plays an enormous part. Of course, you can collect evidence for the manifestation of *seven* in the world *ad infinitum*. For instance, Rom Landau, whom some of you may remember as the author of the interesting book, *God Is My Adventure*, also wrote a book called *Seven*. It has over five hundred pages, and it would not be difficult to double it because our world is simply permeated with the organising figure of seven, both in nature and in man. But, what is perhaps not so obvious, it is also found to be an organising figure in a really comprehensive conception of the evolution of the universe, the earth, and human history. Rudolf Steiner said that one of the first things a disciple in an ancient mystery centre had to learn (and, of course, not just learn in order to know it, but to learn in the sense of absorbing it, understanding it), was to see the organising principle of seven in evolution and history. I want to consider this here because we shall have to refer back to it when we come to the other sevenhoods – the seven seals, the seven trumpets, the seven vials of wrath.

Let me start with the most *comprehensive* chapter. According to Rudolf Steiner, the whole universe goes, at enormous distances of time (and time is hardly any more really a suitable expression) through not only a transformation, but through a stage of returning, dissolving, into sheer energy, and breaking forth again into a manifestation. It goes back into a state which in eastern philosophy is called a *pralaya* state, and then goes forward into a manifestation. Rudolf Steiner describes four ages, what he calls *planetary stages*, or planetary evolutions, of our universe (if you like, reincarnations of our universe), of which the present stage is the fourth. The first one he describes as the *Saturn* stage, the second one as the *Sun* stage, the third one as the *Moon* stage, and then the fourth, what is now our *Earth* stage. The first he describes as consisting entirely of differentiated warmth; after a period of pralaya, the next stage showed differentiation of warmth and air; again after pralaya came the third stage, which he describes as the *Moon* stage, in which, to warmth and air, liquid was added. Then we come into the *Earth* stage where we have firm ground. He speaks of three further stages into which our universe will develop, and this is as far as we can see.

Now, the *Earth* stage, the fourth, similarly itself evolves in seven stages, and at each stage the centre of human activity is at a different place of the globe. The first was the *Polar* stage, when the region of the South Pole was the centre; then the *Hypoborean*; then the *Lemurian*, centred in the southern hemisphere near the present Australia and New Zealand; then the *Atlantean*. The stage we are in now, the fifth, Steiner simply calls the *post-Atlantean*, which is to be followed by two more stages. Again, the post-Atlantean period itself evolves in seven stages which he describes as cultural epochs. The first cultural epoch he calls the *Ancient Indian*; the second, the *Ancient Persian** (with the pre-historic Zarathustra); the third, the *Mesopotamian-Egyptian*; the fourth, the *Graeco-Roman*. The particular

* Both of these refer to pre-historic times.

46

areas so referred to were the centres of these great cultural epochs. Our present epoch, the fifth, Steiner in early days called the Germanic-Anglo Saxon, though later on he no longer used that phrase.

I had to bring this in because, as for a medical student, there comes a time in the study of anatomy when we must also learn the skeleton, which we can then go on to fill again with the whole beauty of the human body, with muscles and veins and arteries, with tissue and nerves etcetera. We shall do so; but we shall really need this 'skeleton' to refer to from time to time. And to close this interlude, I will explain now, for instance, how on the basis of it a certain apocalyptic numerology arises.

Steiner says that we can describe our present age in these terms: 3, 4, 4, because three great planetary evolutions are finished (Saturn, Sun, Moon), four Earth evolutions (Polar, Hypoborean, Lemurian, Atlantean), and four cultural epochs (Ancient Indian, Ancient Persian, Mesopotamian, Graeco-Roman). But this is looking backward. Looking forward, we can write like this: 4, 5, 5, because we are in the fourth great planetary evolution, in the fifth Earth evolution, in the fifth cultural epoch. Now, we can write 6, 6, 6, the famous number of the beast (which you can also read in other ways, as we shall do on another occasion). In the present approach to apocalyptic numerology, this denotes the time when the great, the final decision between good and evil will have to be made – in the sixth planetary evolution, in its sixth age, in the sixth epoch of that age.

I must put these things in because they are involved in the use of numbers in the Book of Revelation, and if we understand the principle of this, we shall also understand that, for instance, in all these sequences of seven the number five has a particular message for us, because we are in two fifth periods: in the fifth period of the great ages of our planet, and in the fifth cultural epoch of the post-Atlantean sub-division. So, for instance, the fifth message, to Sardes, can be read as having a special significance for us. This, again, does not mean that the others are of no interest; but, as we shall see as we go along, in order to make head or tail of such an incredibly complicated and mysterious book, you have to find certain *keys*; you have to find a kind of platform from which you look around. This is where the apocalyptic numerology plays a certain part, and is indeed helpful.

In the message to the angel of the church in Sardes, for instance, there comes this sentence: 'You have a name and you are alive; but in fact you are dead.' It is a very challenging statement: you are supposed to be alive, but you are really dead. These are *key* phrases with which to probe into some of the hidden tendencies and problems of our age. Another reads: 'Strengthen the things that remain.' Do not throw overboard what is still left. This messsage is particularly full with reference to a new manifestation of Christ, a new pressure of Christ on the human soul. And there comes the great challenge: 'Wake up and change your thinking' (generally translated, 'repent', but the Greek for repent is an appeal to *thinking*, not to morality: *metanoeite*). 'If you do not,' the message continues, 'I will come like a thief.' The Greek, then, does not say, 'and you will not know when I shall come', but, 'you will not *have known* when I *have*

48

come'. The event of a fresh Christian element in the world, a Christian presence, *will pass you by*. The effect on your own life will be as if a thief had been and had stolen something, *because you will have missed an opportunity*, because you did not wake up and did not change your mind. These are some of the key phrases from the message to Sardes.

It would be really dogmatic to say that John wrote that, so to speak, for the twentieth century, but, applying the numerology of the Book of Revelation, this is the kind of thing you can do. Here we follow one of Steiner's general suggestions when he says this is not a book which you just read; it is 'ein Übungsbuch', a book for *training*. You have to take certain aspects (and perhaps for a time forget about the rest) and live with them; select those which, for instance, apocalyptic numerology puts before you, and see what they mean. Once you do that, then the book really comes alive, becomes an experience, and not something which you read as a kind of 'sound and fury, signifying nothing' – which is really what it seems to most people.

Now, however, I must return from the seven messages to the original vision – the person or being who instructs John. Remember, he heard the voice from behind:

So I turned round to see what voice it was that was speaking to me. And as I turned I saw seven golden candlesticks, and in the midst of these candlesticks someone in the likeness of a Son of Man. He was clothed in a long robe down to his feet, and with a girdle round his breast. His head and his hair were white like snow-white wool, his eyes like flaming fire, his voice like the sound of rushing waters. He held in his right

49

hand seven stars, and a sharp double-edged sword came out of his mouth. His countenance was like the sun shining in full strength. When I saw him, I fell at his feet like a dead man. But he, laying his right hand upon me, said, 'Do not be afraid. I am he who was at the beginning and shall be at the end, and who lives now. I passed through death, and see, I am alive through all cycles of time. And I hold the keys of death, and of the land of the shades. Write down what you see, what is now, and what will occur hereafter.'

That is the original vision. It is described '*like*' the Son of Man, or *a* Son of Man, a phrase which, in the Gospels, only Christ uses of Himself. No one else ever uses it. It is a really very deep and mysterious phrase, unfortunately a little devalued because it has become religious jargon. It is a kind of integration of the ideal figure of Man (the image of God), lived in, penetrated, and thereby in a way renewed, recreated, by the indwelling Christ.

When one reads this, almost immediately there comes into one's mind a phrase of William Blake (who, as we were reminded by Mr. Harwood last time, was one of the people in more recent times who really lived with the Book of Revelation). He speaks of the '*human form divine*': a wonderful, simple, most telling phrase. Or you may think of the last lines of Coleridge's *Ode to the Departing Year*. After all the turmoil of contemporary history is described, he enters into the silence:

> Now I recentre my immortal mind
> In the deep Sabbath of meek self-content;
> Cleansed from the vapourous passions that bedim
> God's Image, sister of the Seraphim.

Again, there you meet a poetic genius obviously touched

50

by an experience of a similar kind; he sees God's Image – which is Man – 'sister of the Seraphim'.

This is the sort of being John sees. If we consider the many things Rudolf Steiner said in a number of lectures about the Son of Man, we get the impression that for him it was both the archetypal human form as created in the mind of God and, being somehow lost or removed from human life, its restoration by the fact that the Christ used it as the vessel for His Incarnation. It really became *restored* through this combination which last year, speaking of the Baptism, we expressed in the wonderful words of Balfour, when he speaks of Christ's Incarnation as 'the blending of the Glory of Eternity with the Masterpiece of Time'. Through this, the human contribution, the Masterpiece of Time, the most wonderful human figure, was united with the Glory of Eternity, the Christ, thereby *restoring* the Son of Man. This gives a picture which contains, dynamically, the future of Man, and this is what John sees; it is *this* figure which instructs him to write; it is *this* figure which then sets in motion the whole process that culminates in the great split between Babylon and the New Jerusalem. It is this figure in which, really, the secret of Man is contained as he emerges through all these great rounds of seven out of a kind of great cosmic womb, out of a universal mother-spirit, and enters upon an increasing differentiation, practising the apocalyptic virtues of which we read – trial, kingship and patient expectation – and thereby grows from an object of creation into a subject of creation, as a spiritual creative entity, as an individual, as a true ego.

This is foreshadowed, and then in some measure

laid out, in the openings of the seven messages. To conclude, I will draw them together and put them in their essence before us, repeating once more the seven different forms, the seven stages of manifestation of this spiritual being, this Son of Man. Some years ago, I selected the opening sentences of the seven messages and wrote them together, almost in a sort of prayer. It sums up, and yet at the same time it brings this whole sphere down, I might say, within our individual, personal reach, because this is how we might address the Son of Man who is 'the human form divine', and at the same time the image of the Cosmic Christ.

> Thou who holdest the seven stars firmly in thy right hand, and who walkest amidst the seven golden candlesticks; Thou who art the first and the last, who passed through death and hast come alive; Thou who wieldest the sharp two-edged sword; O, Son of God, who hast eyes like flames of fire and feet like white-hot brass, who wieldest the seven spirits of God and the seven stars; Thou holy one, thou real one, who dost hold the key of David which opens and no one shuts, which shuts and no one opens; Thou art the Amen who dost vindicate faith and truth; Thou art the fountainhead and wellspring of the creation of God.

You can make this summary and apply each stage, for instance, to the days of the week. This is a kind of living with the Apocalypse, and you will see how remarkably these seven stages make sense and reveal the esoteric character of the days of the week. Begin, as one does in the esoteric tradition, with Saturday: 'Thou who holdest the seven stars firmly in thy right hand, and who walkest amidst the seven golden candlesticks.' This is the opening sentence that we contemplate on Saturday.

'Thou who art the first and the last, who passed through death and hast come alive': Sunday. One remembers the Resurrection.

'Who wieldest the sharp two-edged sword': Monday, where the split between good and evil, between light and darkness, begins.

'O, Son of God who hast eyes like flames of fire and feet like white-hot brass': Tuesday, where the God of War passes through the world with flaming eyes and flaming feet.

And then the turning point comes on Wednesday, on a new level: 'Who wieldest the seven spirits of God and the seven stars.'

For Thursday, Jupiter day: 'Thou holy one, thou real one, who dost hold the key of David, which opens and no one shuts, which shuts and no one opens.' A kind of priestly function belongs to Jupiter day.

Then for Friday, the day of consummation, the day of love: 'Thou art the Amen who dost vindicate faith and truth; Thou are the fountainhead and wellspring of the creation of God.'

Now if we manage in this sense to bring history and meta-history together, and even bring in an element touching on the personal spiritual life, we move, I believe, in the right direction; we gradually come to grips with the book. We shall never believe or promise that every single detail will be intelligible, but that is not necessary. What we need is a *key* with which to open these locked mansions of the Bible, and perhaps this attempt to have a three-tiered understanding – historical, meta-historical and spiritually personal – is an acceptable attempt to deal with this book, which I hope we shall be able to continue.

The Throne in Heaven and the Heavenly Ritual

When we dealt with the second and third chapters of the Book of Revelation which contain the messages to the seven churches in Asia, we had briefly to introduce numerology. Now I am glad to say, and no doubt most of you will be relieved to hear, that numerology does not play a dominant part in the Book of Revelation; but it does come into it. We cannot ignore it completely because the scheme of the apocalyptic document is built up on sequences of seven, and a few other factors which involve what is generally called numerology. You will remember that I confined myself to a really very brief and almost dogmatic summary of those cosmic and historical periods which according to esoteric tradition, confirmed by Rudolf Steiner on the basis of independent research, play a significant part in the ordering of the evolution of the cosmos and the development of the human race. I am, of course, not going over this whole field again today. I shall disregard the cosmic stages of transformation of our solar system; I shall disregard the various stages of the planetary evolution of our earth; but by way of introduction and linking up with last time, as well as for its own significance, I shall try just once more to bring home to us the significance of the historical periods with which we are perhaps more immediately involved today.

If I may make a personal remark – I was interested in history in a general way very much already as a schoolboy, and during part of my university years I read history, but I was always puzzled by its almost *chaotic* appearance. If we consider nature, we find a quite tangible order; there is seed time and harvest, heat and cold, summer and winter, day and night. If we look up into the sky, we can calculate the movements of the planets, the phases of the moon; we have grasped a quite definite order among the fixed stars. But when we turn to history, there seems to be real chaos – at any rate as a result of the way in which I was taught, and presumably most of you were taught. It seems to be a sequence of wars and famous victories, treaties and covenants (which are broken ten years after although they were declared everlasting at the time they were made), sequences of kings – some of them produced by very doubtful dynastic marriages, and so on and so on. Even if you approach history in a more modern way, as for instance Professor Trevelyan did, and read the *social* history of England from Chaucer to Queen Victoria, you get a picture of history flowing along like a sluggish river, covered with a great deal of flotsam and jetsam, expanding its bed, contracting its bed, but again, rather amorphous, without any kind of structure in it. And so one can understand how one modern school of history has raised the question: Is there a pattern in history? – probably stimulated to start with by Spengler in his *Decline of the West*, which appeared after the First World War, and then further developed by Toynbee

55

and Taylor in Oxford. Is there a *pattern* in history? Some of these historians have tried to find and describe a pattern, and now here in connection with the apocalyptist we can say that he certainly does see a pattern, an order, in history. This pattern is in his view not created by political or economic factors, but by cosmic influences. You may remember that on the first evening* I quoted Rudolf Steiner as saying that history is a *dream* of humanity, that humanity dreams history; and I also quoted Lytton Strachey as saying that *dream* is the essence of history. The writer of the Book of Revelation seems to imply that we dream history also in the sense that we dream these cosmic influences; they stay in our subconsciousness, but they move us to do things, and they *create a pattern* of history.

I should like to illustrate this point with just one really tangible and outstanding example, and you will see then that all this is really relevant to our further study. Historians have been puzzled by the fact that the civilisations of the ancient world all began their chronology, their calendar, their dating, in the third quarter of the eighth century B.C. The Romans dated their history from the foundation of Rome, which they placed at 753 B.C. *Ab urbe condita* ... Everything that happened after that was dated so many years after the foundation of Rome. The Greeks counted their years according to the Olympic Games which took place every four years, and that counting of Olympiads started in 776 B.C. The Assyrians started in 763 and their dating was gradually accepted by all the people in Mesopotamia, and finally even Egypt. Even the Jews,

* See *Answers to Questions*, p. 151.

who were taken into Assyrian captivity in 761, temporarily had to accept this dating. There is even the detail recorded that Hammurahbi, the great king, caused all his clay documents and records prior to this time to be destroyed and an entirely new set of records started.

A reason can be found for this if we follow Rudolf Steiner's indication that at that time a very far-reaching astronomical change took palace – in actual fact a little before, as there is always something of a time-lag between heaven and earth. In 747 the vernal equinox (the point where the sun rises on 21st March) moved from the Bull into the Ram, from Taurus into Aries. It would seem, therefore, that this deliberate starting of a new age with a new calendar, a new chronology, was inspired by and connected with this great cosmic change. You see the fact also reflected in the central ritual symbol of the religions of the time: the movement from the worship of the Bull (Apis, the sacred bull in Egypt, even the Golden Calf) to the Ram: the Ram in the Old Testament and also in Greece. A little earlier, before that date, Zeus transformed himself into a white bull and carried Europa from Asia across the Hellespont into Europe, but after this it was the Golden Fleece, the fleece of the *Ram*, for which the great pilgrimages and voyages were made.*

This is the beginning of one of the historical cycles which are involved and implied in the scheme of the Book of Revelation. Now, it takes the vernal equinox 2,160 years to pass through one sign of the zodiac, in

* Even in the Apocalypse, we could perhaps speak of the *Ram* of God rather than the *Lamb*.

other words, thirty degrees. This was a fact well known to the ancient world: Plato speaks about it, and we know the total length of time for the sun's equinox to move right through the zodiac as the Platonic Year. The time taken by the sun to move through one of these signs is a month in the Platonic Year. So the next change took place 2,160 years later, which is 1413. There is again the time-lag between heaven and earth, but nobody can doubt that round about 1500, although we did not start a new chronology, an entirely new age started – we call it the New Age, the Renaissance, the age of discovery, the new age of learning, the scientific age – that development in which we still find ourselves. If the Book of Revelation speaks of cycles of time, it speaks of cycles of *this* calibre.

Another rather more weighty illustration you see in this volume I have here. Last Saturday was the five hundredth anniversary of the death of the inventor of printing, Johannes Gutenberg, in Mainz. The first book he printed was, of course, the Bible, and the second was a history of the world, known as *The Nuremburg Chronicle*. In honour of this fifth centenary, an American publisher has made a wonderful facsimile edition of this Chronicle of the World, published originally in 1496, and as I have just celebrated an anniversary myself in my life, a good friend gave me this as a birthday present. When you open it you find that it describes the world's history in seven ages. But, it adds, 'When the seventh age is finished, the *last* age.' That is concentrated into only a few pages, with the idea that then we step out of history again and enter into a quite different condition. It goes to show that what I am trying to explain is not just something which Rudolf Steiner tried to get across, or which is the invention of the writer of the Apocalypse, or is some kind of traditional mystical scheme, but something which was *known* to the world until, with the beginning of the New Age, we began to lose sight of these matters. The Elizabethans were still aware of it, and if you want just one further reference to the study of these matters, I recommend Sir Walter Raleigh's *History of the World* – not difficult to read, even in its rather quaint English, and a wonderful book of great information and still having a full grasp, as it were, of the *cosmic pattern of human history*, which people knew they were dreaming, and according to which history made sense and which has provided the basis for understanding that such an ordered sequence of cycles, as in the Book of Revelation, *really was significant*.

The last word I would add is this: that you find a reflection of this even in the Christian ritual of the Communion Service. It is the strange phrase in the Roman Catholic Mass with which so many passages conclude: 'per omnia saecula saeculorum'. That is a ritualistic phrase to convey that what happens there goes on through these periods of periods. Unfortunately in the Anglican ritual it has been replaced by 'world without end', which is one of the not infrequent Jacobean phrases that cover over some of the deeper things no longer understood. If I may say, in the ritual of The Christian Community, which we owe to Rudolf Steiner, the phrase is: 'through all cycles of time', which is perhaps really an adequate modern rendering of this profound conception, that there are *cycles* of time, and they provide the *pattern for history*. We found last time that we ourselves are now in a fifth cycle, characterised by the fact that we confront evil and have death at our elbow. I believe there will not be few among us who will appreciate that this is a very telling description of our age: confrontation with evil, and having death at our elbow. We may therefore take the fifth message, the fifth seal, the fifth trumpet, the fifth vial of wrath as of special significance for our age, as we shall see.

* * *

Having made this link with the matters considered last week, we now turn to our theme for tonight: the throne in heaven and the heavenly ritual. With the next chapters we are for a moment lifted out of history, lifted out of time, into a remarkable heavenly vision. When it begins, we see in little the laws of spiritual cognition of which we spoke on the first evening, which Rudolf Steiner describes invariably in the three stages of Imagination, Inspiration and Intuition: a vision of pictures, a receiving of spiritual hearing and, finally, a confrontation face to face with the substance. At the beginning of this fourth chapter John sees a door is open in heaven; then he hears a mighty voice, saying, 'Come up here', and then, 'immediately I was in the spirit'. The vision of the door, the hearing of the voice, and immediately being in the spirit – you have again the unmistakable sequence of the three stages of spiritual cognition.

And now, that vision. I am really inclined to put the question to you: What is your conception of an abiding presence in the world? Suppose you attended a painting class and your teacher said: Today I'll give you free rein; here are the colours, here are the brushes, here is the piece of paper; now paint what in your opinion expresses something like a really abiding presence in all the changes and vicissitudes of existence. What would you do? I think you (and I) could do worse than paint a throne with something like a brilliance in it. That is precisely what the Book of Revelation presents to us as a vision of an abiding presence, a *Throne in Heaven*, but with no naturalistic description of any figure on that throne — just a blazing brilliance.

> And immediately I was in the spirit; and behold, a throne was set in heaven, and one sat on the throne. And he that sat was to look upon like a jasper and a sardine stone.

These transliterations of the ancient jewel names may be varied, but the impression given is of a stone with a Presence which just *brilliantly* radiates.

This throne rests on translucent crystal. It is described as surrounded up to half its height by what we might call the 'raw material of humanity', the ingredients from which the human being is fashioned. These ingredients are represented by the four *zoa*, the four living creatures (not four *beasts* as the Authorised Version has it). The first is described as an eagle, and in our heads we are in fact 'made of eagle'. If we were beings organised *only* for *thinking* and nothing else, we should all be birds; not that we should necessarily all be eagles, but really birds. The great Greek comic dramatist, Aristophanes, shows that he knew something about this in his play, *The Birds*. If we were bearers *only* of devastating emotions and powerful, aggressive desires, we should all be just lions. The lion region is our chest. If we were given over *only* to digestion and to energising our limbs, we should all be bulls, cattle; we should consume an eighth of our weight in twenty-four hours instead of a fortieth as we actually do, have four stomachs and, nearly all round the twenty-four hours, either guzzle or chew cud. Fortunately, we are not *one* of the three alone; we are all three, together with the fourth of the living creatures who has a face 'as a man'. The fourth principle, the fourth ingredient, holds us together and makes us human beings who, however, still remain akin to the birds in the flight of thought, akin to the lion in the courage and emotions of our heart, and still perhaps powerful and vital in our lower regions and in the movement of our limbs like the bull. There, around the throne, are these four ingredients, this raw material of Man.

If we use for a moment a musical terminology – the first half of the vision is the tonic; the second half provides a kind of dominant, a first attempt at development, because now the radiance begins to operate into the vast darkness around. We are told that the throne is surrounded by a rainbow; the radiance begins to mingle with the darkness and creates colour. There are also seven burning lamps in front of the throne which are the seven Spirits of God. In the beginning of *Genesis* where it says 'God created heaven and earth', there is a plural – not God, but Gods, *Elohim*, and Jewish tradition in the Cabbala (which is the kind of secret teaching alongside the public teaching of the Old Testament) has always taught that the Elohim are seven in number. They are really the Creator Spirits which have brought our universe into being. These seven creative Spirits of God are here represented by the seven torches burning in front of the throne. And, with the twenty-four elders seated round the throne, we come very close to the point where this abiding Presence becomes in a way *pregnant* with activity. They represent the twenty-four cycles of time which have passed since the emergence of the world into existence up to the time of Christ. They will still be there afterwards and be given a new task. Rudolf Steiner calls them in German *die Regler der vierund-zwanzig Weltenstunden* – a wonderful phrase: 'the regulators of the twenty-four hours of the cosmic clock'. There they sit.

And now this vision is summed up by the description of the whole company that surrounds the throne bursting into a kind of song, into a kind of acclamation:

> Thou art worthy O lord to receive glory and honour and power: for thou hast created all things, and for thy pleasure they are and were created.

I think one can make the three substantives used here a little more understandable. In my own translation I have developed the thought a little by saying:

> Thou art worthy, O lord, to receive *the* glory *of life, the* dignity *of soul* and *the* power *of spirit,*

because it is these three spheres which are referred to here. Of life the best you can say is that it is *glorious*, which means both glorious in the sense in which we use it, and radiating. The highest achievement of a human soul development is honour, *dignity*. And the highest achievement of spirit is *spirit power* – at any rate in this context.

This hymn, as you may call it, has caused some theological and historical scholars to put forward a quite interesting theory. They have discovered that these phrases occur in the ritual of Caesar-worship. You may remember I mentioned last time that in the place of one of the seven churches in Asia, Pergamum, Caesar-worship was first started. There Augustus was first proclaimed as a god, as divine, and there the actual ritual, nine years before Christ, was started. In the message to Pergamum we have the characteristic sentence: 'I know thy works, and where thou dwellest, even where Satan's seat is.' Historians have been intrigued by the idea that it might be a reference to the beginning of Caesar-worship. At the same time, Pergamum prided itself on the most magnificent altar of Zeus in the ancient world.* An alternative idea is that 'Satan's seat' may refer to this altar of Zeus. Very likely both things come together; though not entirely established, we may take the hypothesis that the first acclamation of Augustus as a god took place in that setting. The *acclamatio* is actually preserved and it begins: *Vere dignus es* (Thou art very worthy to be called) – *Deus ac Dominus Augustus* (God and Lord Augustus).

In this verse, therefore, we have really a parallel to the actual ritual of Caesar-worship. The orthodox ex-

* This enormous monument has been excavated and put up in Berlin. It has friezes all round it and stands on a huge platform approached by marble steps. I have always taken a particular interest in it because the leader of that expedition which unearthed it, attached to the German Archaeological Institute, the late Professor Andrae, was a very prominent member of the Anthroposophical Movement and also of The Christian Community in Berlin. It is now in the eastern half of the city, but quite unscathed, and is really worth visiting.

planation has been that John, or whoever wrote the Apocalypse, put this in as a kind of counter-blast to Caesar-worship; instead of Caesar, it is the One who sits on the throne, it is the Divine Presence, who is 'vere dignus', who is 'Deus ac Dominus' etcetera. It is taken as a kind of polemic antidote to Caesar-worship. I very much doubt that that *is* the sequence of events, the right description of cause and effect. I believe the true case is that the vision presented in that chapter of the throne in heaven and all that goes with it is the original, *primal* vision known to the initiates of all ages, and that from that primal, archetypal vision the priests of the ancient world took down and adopted certain sequences and phrases for the worship of their priest-kings – the Pharaohs, the great kings of Persia and Assyria and, finally, the Caesars. It is not John who copies Caesar-worship: Caesar-worship, perhaps second hand, or third hand, copies the divine ritual. The *original* vision is here attained by the man who saw the door, who heard the voice and was finally 'immediately in the spirit'.

When you read that song at the end of the fourth chapter, you become aware of an increasing tension. I have said already the situation is, as it were, pregnant with something which *must now happen*. The abiding Presence is *so* charged with activity, with power, that it cannot just remain. It *must act*, create for its own pleasure, so to speak, out of its *love* to do things. And this is now described in the next chapter in a very dramatic way. There the cosmic tension is perhaps to start with even enhanced through a new symbol which appears – the book, the scroll with seven seals. Suddenly John sees it 'in the right hand of him that sat on the throne'. That is the next stage. At that moment, a tremendous cosmic challenge sounds through the spiritual world, uttered by a mighty angel, who is not given any name in this particular context – we might surmise who it is, but perhaps we will leave him unmentioned for the moment. He shouts with a loud voice: 'Who is worthy to open the book and to loose the seals thereof?' I would here refer to a telling phrase from the book by Emil Bock on the Apocalypse.* He says there was a danger that 'eternal duration might have become cosmic stagnation'. It is for this reason that the angel cries out and calls through heaven this cosmic challenge: 'Who is worthy to break the seals?' This is what makes things happen.

We then see how deeply John is involved. He cannot bear the silence; there is no answer, nothing happens to start with, and so he says, 'I wept bitterly.' This personal involvement of John in the Apocalypse distinguishes the whole book – we shall see that a little more closely next time – from the great mass of apocalyptic literature which existed in the two hundred years before Christ and the hundred years afterwards. There is great personal and active involvement of the seer himself. He weeps bitterly. Then one of the elders comes and tries to comfort him (perhaps the last of the twenty-four hours of the cosmic clock, the one who led right up to the time of Christ) and says: 'Weep not: behold the Lion of the tribe of Judah has prevailed to open the book and to loose the seven seals thereof.' John looks, and sees in the centre of the throne not a lion but the Lamb. It is one of the most moving

* *The Apocalypse of St. John*, Emil Bock, The Christian Community Press, London, 1957.

transformations in the whole book. His attention is drawn to a *lion*, and he looks to see that tremendous, powerful being who will now set evolution in motion, and, instead of a lion, he sees a lamb. And there, in this picture, you see the great reality: that the greatest force is not the wild, untamed force of the lion, but the force of sacrifice, of love. This is really the highest magic which can now set things in motion.

The four living beings and the twenty-four elders sing again a kind of acclamation, but now it is a new song. Then for the first time the angels join in, in all their masses. 'The number of them was ten thousand times ten thousand, and thousands of thousands' — myriads and myriads in the original Greek. It is a wonderful idea that now, when the whole thing is set in motion, *all* the heavenly hierarchies begin to take an interest. It needed the Lamb to be there for the seal to be broken, for evolution to begin out of cosmic duration into dynamic activity, and at that moment the hierarchies are at hand. Now they sing a *new* song, and their new song is not confined to the three virtues: the glory of life, the dignity of soul, the power of spirit, but (and I read them now simply as they stand in the Authorised Version, leaving it to go into more deeply next time) now it says: 'Worthy is the Lamb that was slain to receive power, and riches, and wisdom, and strength, and honour, and glory, and blessing.' We shall see that these are the fundamental virtues of the sevenfold being of Man as he will develop, with the help and the power of the Lamb, into the fullness of his cosmic nature.

*   *   *

This is how the fifth chapter closes. And we may now look at these two chapters describing the vision of the throne and the heavenly ritual within the structure of the whole book. In the sixth chapter the first seal will be opened, followed by the others, and therewith the apocalyptic tests and trials begin. Simply from the viewpoint of spiritual-literary structure, I think it is a wonderful fact that before we enter into what I have called in the next lecture's title 'the necessity of doom', the necessity of trials and tests and sufferings, we are allowed this vision; we are allowed to take a deep breath of this heavenly atmosphere, which should go with us on our pilgrimage. It has been said that this approach shows the patience of God with man; He allows man first of all to saturate himself in, and to assure himself of, the abiding spiritual Presence before he has to descend into the depths and take on his destiny, his karma, his trials, his tests, and even taste of doom. I think that is a rather wonderful conception: whatever happens now, we should remember that there is this abiding Presence in the spiritual world, like the sun which shines even if below there are clouds and foul weather which hide it from us. Perhaps I may use a rather starkly materialist parable, which comes quite fittingly to our age. No doubt many of you have travelled by plane and left on a day when it was very wet and foul below, and in a few minutes were above the clouds to find the sun in the blue sky. Sometimes you can see the shadow of the plane on the clouds below and it is surrounded by the circular halo of a rainbow – a magnificent spectacle. Perhaps it is not too bad to take such a picture and turn it into a spiritual symbol; we may take it for the experience which is vouchsafed to us in chapters four and five. Above the clouds, which are inevitable – they are part of the climate of our existence, like the tests and trials of the emotional world, the emotional clouds – above them there *is* the sun shining for ever, there *is* the throne, and the raw material of Man, there *are* the great guides of the cosmic cycles, and the celestial hierarchies, there *is* the Lamb giving His power of sacrifice and of love.

There is no doubt that in times of real personal trial and trouble this is a magnificent vision to contemplate. It carries conviction almost immediately; and I believe it will be quite good to end this study by saying that if we need serenity at a time of trouble it is very helpful to contemplate this wonderful vision of the throne in heaven and the heavenly ritual.

Questions and answers were recorded after this lecture. See p. 153.

The Freedom of Redemption and the Necessity of Doom

The Book of Revelation is not the only apocalyptic document in existence. A number of apocalyptic writings has been preserved and handed down. Scholars even speak of apocalyptic writing as a specific literary form, a form of writing that deals with hidden things and prophesies events yet hidden in the future. It is a kind of literary form which in modern terms we would call a combination of occult science and prophecy. Canon Philips writes in the preface to his interesting new translation of the Book of Revelation: 'Books of revelation or apocalypses were common in Jewish literature in times of national persecution. And this Christian apocalypse closely follows the form and style of such writings.' The Book of Revelation certainly follows the style and form of Jewish apocalypses fairly closely, but the first part of the sentence is a generalisation which is not quite correct, because books of revelation were written *only* within a period of three hundred years – two hundred years before Christ and one hundred years after Christ. And it is a remarkable fact that never before and never after were such books written. Incidentally, the discovery of the Dead Sea Scrolls has added a few more apocalyptic documents to our knowledge.

The reason for this is worth studying because it also

partly helps us to understand the mental background to the book itself. We must imagine, of course, that St. John and people of his time had a quite distinct experience of human evolution. I say advisedly 'experience of evolution' and not 'theory', because they had no theories. *We* have theories. Darwin's presentation of evolution is a theory. He collected many facts, but he presented a *theory*, and quite rightly we speak of the theory of evolution, not of the *experience* of evolution. But in those days people had an experience of evolution which told them that humanity had descended from an earlier and more spiritual form of existence into a later and more material form of existence. For instance, in the matter of sleeping and waking the difference is very marked. In the earliest forms of human evolution human souls were really awake during sleep and were active as spirits among spirits, both in cognition and action, and when they woke up they returned into the warm nest of the physical body and rested. That is why we have so few traces of early material civilisation; men confined their physical activity to the absolute minimum necessary to satisfy their material needs. At night, however, they were awake and active and moved as spirit among spirits. This gradually changed. The night mind became darkened, obscured and finally completely unconscious as it is with us today, and the day mind woke up, man's eyes were opened and he began to see the material world, saw it increasingly 'naked', without its spiritual counterpart; in the end, to his surprise and shock, he saw even himself naked, without aura, without spiritual counterpart; he became fully awakened to the sense perception as we have it today.

Now this 'descent', this darkening of man's relationship to his spiritual home, was the price he paid for the awakening to the surrounding material world; it was well known and felt, and by no means only in the Jewish tradition. The classical writers, Greek and Roman, spoke of the various ages: the Golden Age, the Silver Age, the Bronze Age, and finally they felt the Iron Age had arrived, a brutal age in which the gods withdrew and in which, as they said, Truth, Beauty and Goodness veiled their faces and also vanished among the Olympians. The Teutonic people spoke of the Twilight of the Gods, of the death of Baldur. In Egypt, Isis lost her husband, and her son was murdered. In this country the Druidic religion fell into that state of decadence of which Julius Caesar writes in some passages. It is really an interesting historical observation (which is generally overlooked in the ordinary study of history) that during the last two hundred years before Christ this *darkening* of the inward scene took place and became almost complete. While the Romans outwardly conquered one nation after another, and carried their leaders in triumph through Rome, sensitive souls felt on the *inward* plane that the end of the world had come, the doom had arrived when man had finally lost membership of the spiritual world, had finally been separated from the gods. The classic, the typical, expression of this sense of doom is contained in the apocalyptic writing, the expressions of what one might call even the apocalyptic movement. In Biblical terms, it covers the period from Daniel (the Book of Daniel can fairly well be dated as between about 160 and 170 B.C.) to the time of our Book of Revelation, which is, in a way, a climax, the consummation of the apocalyptic movement and the apocalyptic writing.

Our book, *the* Apocalypse, however, stands out for a number of specific characteristics. First of all, of course, it makes the unique claim that it is the apocalypse of Jesus Christ which God gave to John. (You may remember the Jacob's ladder of descent we presented on the first evening: from God, to Christ, to the Angel, to John, to the reader, to the listeners and, finally, to those who pondered the content.) This is a unique claim. And, of course, alone it would not carry weight if we did not gradually see in the book's whole spirit, in its whole content, how this claim is borne out.

While all the other apocalyptic writings, including those, and particularly those in the Jewish tradition, but not exclusively so, add to their description of tragedy and doom just a spark of Messianic hope (among these writings is, for instance, also included Virgil's famous Fourth Eclogue, promising the birth of a child), our Book of Revelation speaks of the *coming* Christ. Right at the beginning it opens with a reference – 'see he comes in the clouds; and all generations shall see him, even those who have pierced him: all human souls shall be shaken to the depths' – 'shall wail' the Authorised Version says. This vision of the Christ on the clouds appears repeatedly in the book; in one remarkable context, He is described sitting on the cloud with a sickle and presiding over the harvest of the earth, the harvest of humanity. And in order really to bring the Book of Revelation somewhat nearer to our immediate level, I must still by way of introduction say a word about this picture and this reference to the clouds.

The Biblical documents referring to clouds speak not only of the physical clouds we see in the sky, but of cloud of a different kind – the invisible cloud that surrounds all living things, the radiation of life, the etheric aura of living things; this is also *nephele*, is also a cloud. And if we follow Steiner's lead in these matters, we may expect a new presence and a new activity of the living Christ in this world of the living clouds, in this world of etheric reality, in the world of life. This presence is not a static one, not one which manifests itself once and then ceases, but which manifests itself, as all life does, in rhythms. There are periods of human evolution when this presence of Christ in the world of life becomes activated (in religious terms one often speaks of His pressure on human souls increasing); and there are periods when it recedes and allows the human race as it were to go on for a bit by itself, under its own steam. The Book of Revelation speaks rather more specifically to ages in which this pressure from the clouds increases, and perhaps it would hardly be dogmatic to say, as it is pretty obvious, that we are finding ourselves in a century when such a pressure can be increasingly felt, all the more so because on the ordinary level of history the original light, the original impulse of Christianity, is gradually dying out and vanishing. We experience something like the *doom* which the apocalyptists felt in their own time, but on the other hand, this renewed pressure, this renewed presence in the field of life, in the etheric realm. Taking this, perhaps, only as an hypothesis, giving it the benefit of the doubt, we might feel that the Book of Revelation speaks quite

74

specifically to our condition. Hitherto, we have refrained from making it in this sense topical, but now I think we can. Now we can give it the benefit of the doubt that it speaks of things that concern us; our business, our concerns are transacted in the book.

*   *   *

Now let us turn to the book itself and once more take a comprehensive view of it. The book moves, to use its own phrase, from *Alpha* to *Omega*. Teilhard de Chardin, who is so earnestly studied by spiritual seekers today, speaks about the omega point to which the whole creation moves, and speaks about this omega point in very moving terms. But he is somewhat vague about the alpha point, the origin, the beginning of it all, the dynamic content of it all, what it is all about. Why do we move towards Omega? The Book of Revelation provides the omega point, of course, in the picture of the New Jerusalem, but it provides the alpha point in that first great vision which John receives on the Lord's day on Patmos, when he finds himself in the spirit. There, he sees the Son of Man with 'human form divine', but this 'human form divine', this vision, carries among its various character-istics one particularly important one, one which has its direct relation to the omega point. Here, for once, I will read a fairly long quotation from Rudolf Steiner, from the opening of the eighth lecture of his cycle on the Apocalypse, which he gave in 1908 in Nuremburg.* The opening pages of the lecture deal with this dynamic quality of the alpha point and, in a

* Rudolf Steiner, *The Apocalypse of St. John*, Rudolf Steiner Press, London, 1977.

75

sense, decode one of the principal symbols of the Book of Revelation.*

We have now progressed so far in our considerations that we have seen what a sharp two-edged sword this ego of man is. Those who do not fully realise that this ego is a two-edged sword will scarcely be able to grasp the entire meaning of the evolution of mankind and the world. On the one hand this ego is the cause that man hardens within himself, and that he desires to draw into the service of his ego his inner capacities and all the outer objects at his disposal. This ego is the cause of man's directing all his wishes to the satisfaction of this ego as such. Its striving to draw to itself as its own possession a part of the earth which belongs to all, to drive away all the other egos from its realm, to fight them, to be at war with them, is one side of the ego. But on the other hand we must not forget that it is the ego that at the same time gives man his independence and his inner freedom, which in the truest sense of the word exalts him. His dignity is founded in this ego, it is the basis of the divine in man.

This conception of the ego presents difficulties to many people. It has become clear to us that this ego of man has developed from a group-soul nature, from a kind of all-inclusive universal ego out of which it has been differentiated. It would be wrong if man were to crave to go down again with this ego into some sort of universal consciousness, into some sort of common consciousness. Everything which causes a man to strive to lose his ego and dissolve it into a universal consciousness is the result of weakness. He alone understands the ego who knows that after he has gained it in the course of cosmic evolution it cannot be lost; and above all man must strive for the strength (if he understands the mission of the world) to make this ego ever more inward, ever more divine. True anthroposophists possess nothing of the empty talk which continually emphasises the dissolution of the ego in a universal self, the melting into some sort of primeval gruel. True Anthroposophy can only put forward as

* Rev. I:16.

76

the final goal the community of free and independent egos, of egos which have become individualised. It is just this that is the mission of the Earth, which is expressed in love, that the egos learn to confront one another freely. No love is perfect if it proceeds from coercion, from people being chained together. Only when each ego is so free and independent that it need not love, is its love an entirely free gift. It is the divine plan to make this ego so independent that as an individual being in all freedom it can offer love even to God. It would amount to man being led by strings of dependence if he could in any way be forced to love, even if only in the slightest degree.

Thus the ego will be the pledge for the highest goal of man. But at the same time, if it does not discover love, if it hardens within itself, it is the tempter that plunges him into the abyss. Then it becomes what separates men from one another, what brings them to the great War of All against All, not only the war of nation against nation (for the conception of a nation will then no longer have the significance it possesses today) but to the war of each single person against every other person in every branch of life; to the war of class against class, caste against caste, and sex against sex. Thus in every field of life the ego will become the bone of contention; and hence we may say that it can lead on the one hand to the highest and on the other hand to the lowest. For this reason it is a sharp two-edged sword. And He who brought the full ego-consciousness to man, Christ Jesus, is, as we have seen, symbolically and correctly represented in the Apocalypse as one who has the sharp two-edged sword in his mouth.

Incidentally, this is perhaps the most classical description in Steiner's lectures of the human ego in its complete, clear, double nature – the two-edged sword.

Going now from *this* alpha point to the omega point, we can understand how, at the end of the Book of Revelation, we are presented with a two-edged civilisation – the civilisation of Babylon and the civilisation of Jerusalem. Between this Alpha and Omega lies the whole dynamic unfolding of human development, and it is by no means accidental that both Jerusalem and Babylon are presented as women. Altogether in the ancient civilisations, cities were regarded as feminine. It implied the perhaps instinctive knowledge that the individual ego is of a masculine quality whether it lives in a man or a woman (we shall hear more about that when we speak of the war in heaven where the woman clothed with the sun brings to birth the male principle), but is brought to its development, to its rounding off and fullness by the feminine element, represented by the community, the city. Babylon is represented as that scarlet woman quality which *grabs*, which demands, which takes advantage, which takes and takes and takes; and we shall see in the last lecture all the things she takes, culminating in the taking of the bodies and souls of men. That is, as Steiner says, the quality that plunges humanity into the abyss. On the other hand there is the Jerusalem quality, that of the bride who loves. The beauty of that is expressed in those wonderful documents we get from the ancient world, like Plato's *Symposium*, with all its transformation from Eros into Agape without the kind of dividing line, without, at least, a curtain between the two, or in Goethe's *Faust* – the eternal feminine in Gretchen going through love and tragedy to the final redemption where she can welcome Faust, at the end of his pilgrimage, into heaven.

These fundamental mysteries, which are the concern of every man and woman, every human soul alive, are there in the Book of Revelation. Between these alpha and omega points a whole panorama of imagery

78

is displayed. If we then take the book and begin to read chapter after chapter, verse after verse, once, twice, three times, seven times, we shall probably come to the humble conclusion that we are not likely to understand a great deal of it. It is written in code. We should not be surprised if we took up a book on chemistry full of formulae and did not understand it unless we studied chemistry, or took up a book on mathematical physics with all its equations and were puzzled, and the Book of Revelation belongs to that sort of category; it has to be decoded, and that is not very quickly done. But, a broad reading, as I have implied, would give us at any rate one first comprehensive impression, surprising and challenging and disquieting, that the verses and chapters dealing with tragedies, with doom, with horrors, are far more numerous than the comparatively limited and rare chapters dealing with salvation, liberation and redemption. But what is to us surprising was not surprising to John and men of his age with their general outlook on the world and on history.

John took seriously the beginning of *Genesis*, the story of the Fall, the poison of the magic apple and all that followed. As we know, if someone takes poison, we can fairly well anticipate that he will be seriously sick, suffer all kinds of horrible symptoms and may have to take a very nasty medicine. This 'necessity of doom' – to use the phrase of our title – is quite understandable to us in such a case. And so it was understandable to John – humanity *had* taken poison; there is therefore a certain inbuilt necessity of doom operating. On the other hand, supposing we take a tonic and are going to feel the better tomorrow, the day after tomorrow, it would be very much more difficult to say what we are then going to do, because we operate *then* in freedom. Deeds of freedom, constructive deeds of freedom, cannot be prophesied, simply because they *are* free, and not even an Almighty God can know beforehand what a truly free human being is going to do. That implies a concept of freedom which is not based on a philosophical argument whether we are or not, but based on the experience that at certain moments, perhaps rare moments, we *are* free. Most of the time we are not, but there are moments when we act neither under the coercion of our nature, nor in conformity with convention, but deal with a set of circumstances quite constructively and artistically. At that moment we have the profound experience which goes right through the body – all its bones and all its muscles and all its veins and all its arteries – that *we are free*. These are rare events, but what we do, and what humanity does in those moments, is *not* the subject of prophecy. So we have this remarkable relationship: on the one hand chapters describing 'the necessity of doom', and on the other comparatively few chapters speaking of freedom, the possible freedom, of redemption, of salvation. I will first deal briefly with the two chapters which are interspersed like islands of liberation: chapters seven and fourteen – characteristic numbers.

Chapter seven begins by telling us that there is now a moment when the angels who control certain great catastrophes on earth are told to hold their hand because something quite different is to take place now. The cosmic storm is stilled, the winds in the four corners of the earth are held back, and now those called 'the servants of God' are 'sealed'. Something is done to them; a seal is impressed, a passport is given them. The servants of God are integrated with the spiritual direction of humanity. Then we are told there are a hundred and forty-four thousand of them, not a difficult number to understand – twelve times twelve. Here we have a principle of spiritual or occult sociology, that twelve is the symbol of the perfect number for an individual human community. Christ had twelve disciples, King Arthur had twelve knights, and, further back, in the time when this was more a matter of the blood-tie, Jacob had twelve sons. We find this number of twelve as the figure of an ideal community. (Rudolf Steiner said that if there is a thirteenth he is a repetition of one of those already present.) The ideal organisation of potential communities is again a matter of twelve; and so with the ideal pattern of twelve times twelve, we circumscribe, as it were, the cornerstone, the crystallising point, of organised humanity of the future.

The hundred and forty-four thousand are first described, and then after this we read that masses of people from all nations and tongues and tribes and races stand before the throne because that cornerstone is first formed. And now we are given in a picture one of those interludes when we can look from the valley of the shadow of death, where doom prevails, on to an island of liberation; and there are certain social, spiritual organisational laws for these servants of God. The cry which they utter 'with a loud voice' is translated: 'Salvation to our God which sitteth upon the throne'. Why should God need salvation? Literally, what you can understand from the Greek is: 'Healing (*soteria*) belongs to God.' *All* the things described in the book are medicine, are healing. The mischief was done in Paradise; now comes healing.

Now also all the angels round about the throne worship God saying,

> Amen: Blessing, and glory, and wisdom, and thanksgiving, and honour, and power, and might, be unto our God for ever and ever. Amen.

I do not know whether on hearing this read you have noticed that there are seven attributes pronounced. To start with, perhaps, one cannot make a great deal of it, but, since there are seven, of course one goes back to it as one of the keys for study. From a study of the Greek and out of an anthroposophical background, you come to the conclusion that what the hosts in heaven sing, what they pronounce as a sequence of seven, are the seven ideal qualities for the sevenfold human being. Now Steiner describes the human being, as we know it normally among us on earth, as having a physical body, that physical body permeated by a life-body (which he has in common with the plants), in turn permeated by his soul or astral body (which he has in common with the animals), and then by what makes man, man – his spiritual self, his ego – the two-edged sword. But then Steiner describes how in the future man will unfold himself still further and gradually transform these life forces, these soul forces, these spirit forces, into three higher beings of man, for which he sometimes uses terms of eastern philosophy: Manas, Budhi, Atma.

If we take this into consideration, we have in these seven words the seven ideal qualities applicable to the sevenfold being of man – reading not from the bottom upwards, from the physical to the spirit man, but from the top downwards. *Eulogia*, blessing, is the highest that man's transformed physical body, as Spirit-Man, Atma, can achieve. Then we come to the transformed etheric body, the Budhi, the Life-Spirit; its quality is *doxa*, glory, radiance. Further down is what will develop just above our Ego, the higher soul-being, the Spirit-Self, Manas; its content, its finest achievement, is wisdom, *sophia*. Then comes the ego, and *eucharistia*, thanksgiving or self-giving, is its highest ideal; the self grows by giving itself. Coming further down into the soul region, or astral body, *timé*, dignity, is the highest quality. Of the life-body, or etheric body, *dynamis*, vitality, is the best quality, and then, finally, of the physical body, *ischys*, strength, power, stability. So, in such a hymn which otherwise seems rather like celestial sound and fury signifying nothing, we can discover some real content.

In this seventh chapter, then, we find the servants of God occupied in describing their position in this way. They sing a song representing the unfolding of man in his full sevenfold quality; they sing of the healing power of God. They are organised in a twelvefold way, and we can understand if we are also told that they are dressed in white garments (the Greek really says a white garment is thrown around them), and that they carry palms as the symbol of victory.

In chapter fourteen, the other mountain of liberation, we see the one hundred and forty-four thousand again; now they are not given a seal, but they have the name of the Lamb and of His Father on their foreheads. To some extent they have assimilated what has been given to them and it is now more within them. Now, too, there is one quite new quality, because they sing a new song. You could also translate it 'a song of renewal'. And that song of renewal is accompanied by harps. This is the famous passage where the book, so wonderful in its musical poetry, says: 'I heard the voice of harpers harping on their harps' – a literal translation of the Greek. (This, of course, is the passage that has given material for so many friendly jokes about the occupation in heaven, and even the boredom to do with it.)

In his book on the Apocalypse, Emil Bock* makes the following observation at this point:

> The Trumpets have played their part in the great world orchestra; the conductor beckons them to retire. For a little while they are still heard in the distance. Thunder rolls through the cosmos like an echo dying away. But no silence follows. Enchanting strains are heard. As quiet undertones they were already sounding before, but they had been drowned by the noise of the Trumpets. It is the sound of harps.

The whole context shows that at this stage (it is a further stage, now) the humanity sharing in this freedom begins to learn to play an instrument in which the ancient harmony of the spheres can be reflected and received. We shall have to speak of the harmony of the spheres in another context, so I leave it for the moment at this remark. The new song indicates that they are *involved* in, joining in, the world harmony, which is a kind of counterpoint to the noise which history makes; it belongs to the abiding vision really,

* *The Apocalypse of St. John*, Emil Bock, The Christian Community Press, London, 1957.

84

yet is not static, but creative. Man learns now to become a creator, to add to the creating sounds that keep the universe going.

Having looked at these two islands of liberation, we shall now have courage to look at the flood of doom which fills the chapters on which we concentrate tonight, from six to ten. Obviously, from these chapters we can select only a few outstanding symbols with which perhaps we are somehow more familiar than with others.

In the sixth chapter the first seal is opened, and then we have a quick sequence of the four apocalyptic horsemen. What do they represent? I shall now be a little dogmatic. In the ancient civilisations, the horse, and particularly the head of the horse, was a symbol for earthly intelligence (one might note our expression 'horse-sense'). The four apocalyptic horsemen in their quick succession describe in pictorial form the gradual transformation and, in a sense, descent, of the earthly intellect. First the white horse: the intellect is still pure and the rider is an archer; he hits the mark. The next one is a red horse; the intellect is beginning to serve the emotions, the voice of the blood, and therefore the second rider has a sword; he starts war, fighting between men. The third one is black; the intellect becomes very black and material, and the rider is given balances and measures. He begins to measure the world and express it entirely in terms of weight and figure and size, representative of a mechanical world picture. And then the last stage is revealed by the fourth rider on a putrid horse (not a 'pale' horse, in the Greek); the intellect becomes cynical. Death rides it and Hades, the underworld, follows it.

Without wishing to be too dramatic, I think there is a lot in this that we can understand; we have reached that stage where the intellect has become almost putrid. We analyse everything, we kill it, and the underworld, the subhuman world, begins to show its activity.

The seventh chapter we have already described as one of the islands of liberation. In the eighth chapter the seventh seal is opened and the trumpets sound, and always a third of that part of creation mentioned is destroyed. This I should like to hold over till we consider the war in heaven, but as far as the actual destruction goes, I shall come back to it at the end of this talk.

In chapter nine the fifth trumpet sounds and there we are met with some of the strange apocalyptic pictures. Out of the smoke, locusts come upon the earth,

> and unto them was given power, as the scorpions of the earth have power . . . And the shapes of the locusts were like unto horses prepared unto battle; and on their heads were as it were crowns like gold, and their faces were as the faces of men . . . And thus I saw the horses in my vision, and them that sat on them, having breastplates of fire . . . and the heads of the horses were as the heads of lions, and out of their mouths issued fire and smoke and brimstone . . . For their power is in their mouth and in their tails; for their tails were like unto serpents, and had heads, and with them they do hurt.

What are we to make of these pictures? We must be willing to grasp the idea that John, the apocalyptist, does not see only with physical eyes, but with spiritual eyes. He sees human beings in their physical condition, but also in their soul condition. He is clairvoyant; he sees the aura. And it is simply a fact that, at certain times, although perhaps they are always there, these things reach a climax. There *are* human beings on earth who in their aura look as these creatures are described. Very early on in my life as a young man, I had an experience which I will not describe in detail but which has given me an insight into this world, and I have known ever since that what is written here is true. Rudolf Steiner himself also described such things here and there, and with particular reference to these pictures says: 'Here we have the description of human beings who in their soul-nature *look* like this, and, of course, have the effect on other people which is described here.' He also said that, looked at with the eye of the clairvoyant, most of us to this day appear still as centaurs. In our aura we are *not* entirely human; we are human down to the waist, and below we are centaurs. This is the general condition of humanity at this stage, and only gradually do we emerge from that situation. The terrifying creatures that are described in the Book of Revelation are variations on this.

Perhaps one need not really labour the point. If one reads the book, one simply comes up against these things, and in one sense perhaps one is shocked and in another grateful to find such remarks of Rudolf Steiner because one sees there is sense in what the book describes. It is not necessary now to go very much more into detail (in the next two or three lectures we shall have to deal with the grim side of the book considerably more), but try, in conclusion, once more to establish a kind of general human relationship to these dark pictures.

I can speak only for myself and for a few friends

with whom I occasionally discuss these matters, but it seems to be (and I should be interested to hear what you feel) that if one reads this book, strangely enough one feels almost more at home in what I would like to call 'the valley of decision' than on 'the mount of liberation'. And that is not only modesty that one cannot see oneself in a white garment joining the people with the palms in their hands; there is something quite deep down in one's nature wherein one feels there is something *right*, even if one does not understand the detail of this sequence of dangerous and terrible things. G. K. Chesterton expressed that feeling once in a homely way when he said: 'I like getting into hot water; it keeps me clean.' In a homely way, you can feel this on reading some of these terrifying chapters. They *are* boiling hot water. But, presumably, they are meant to keep us clean.

We have among the regular attenders of these Tuesday evenings, a distinguished modern painter whose illustrations to the Book of Revelation were published by Collins. He kindly leant me his copy of the book and I looked through it with great interest and was deeply impressed. What struck me particularly was that, although there are the angels and all that belongs to heaven, *all* the illustrations give the impression that this painter, painting out of the mentality of our century, *really must express* the abiding reality of these terrible things, even at the end when John is taken by the angel upon a mountain; he is painted wringing his hands, watching from across the valley the coming of the New Jerusalem. Obviously he wrings his hands partly in joy, and yet you get the impression that he takes a deep breath; he has gone through it all, and he would never, never be able to enjoy that sight of the New Jerusalem if he had not gone through the depths before. That was absolutely necessary. And, you see, there is that sense in which tragedy, challenge, suffering are more real than easy enjoyment.

This is something expressed also by thinkers and artists in other media. We could take, for example, Anouilh's modern adaptation of Sophocles's *Antigone*, in which one factor strongly brought out is that for Antigone the only *real* thing, which she can sense with a sense of reality, is *death*. Everything else is window dressing and vain show; we live with it, but it is – in eastern terms – it is *maya*. It is very enjoyable, but the only *reality* is the confrontation with death. And this is the atmosphere, the conviction, the *sense* of part of the Apocalypse. Therefore it is a tonic. Some of you may remember the peculiar gift that Winston Churchill had during the war of making all the austerities and war regulations sound *not* as if they were simply austerities and restrictions, but a kind of national tonic.

This is what the Book of Revelation *really* can do, but now, in order to accept that, we must just share one last thought. Even accepting this approach which I recommend, you may still say that it is very grim indeed that about a third of the world of man should be destroyed and dropped into the lake of fire etcetera. This is really very difficult to grasp, but Rudolf Steiner gives a very simple lead by saying you must distinguish between individual and race. And by race, in this context, he does not mean what we normally think of as race – black, white, brown etcetera, but he means groups, sections of humanity, particular types of humanity, even perhaps distinguished by certain subtle physiological peculiarities or other difficulties, or perhaps not even noticeably different. And then you must bring to bear on it (although this is not directly explained in the book) the idea of reincarnation, because obviously this great drama cannot be understood, or lived, or be taken into consideration, if you think in terms of one human life only. But if you take that vast vista, which becomes rapidly familiar to an increasing number of people and which is implied in the book, then you can understand Steiner's lead when he says there will be certain types of humanity destroyed; they will have no offspring. Putting things very crudely in my own words – there will be times when there are many human individualities in the spiritual world and only the strongest, those who have made the biggest spiritual strides, will be able to form a body and be born on the earth and continue human evolution on earth. The ordinary Christian might say: 'Wonderful – and the rest of us can stay in heaven!' But that would not be wonderful, because it is *deeply* built into the human soul that its mission is to advance and cultivate and transform this planet; and to be in the spiritual world without a chance to come to earth must give a sense of terrible disappointment and frustration, in *cosmic* dimensions. We talk of frustration here and we know what it is, but think of frustration of a cosmic size: that is suffering. Only those who are strong enough will come and continue to work and carry on human evolution, and make it gradually possible for others to come. But that really needs heroic souls, and the Book of Revelation is a handbook, a training book, for heroic souls, not for those who feel they would like to be able to say they 'have never had it so good'.

This leads me in conclusion to quote a few sentences from Soloviev's *Antichrist*. He was one of the most interesting and original of Russian thinkers, who died in 1901. He describes the Antichrist as the great *benefactor* of humanity, who rescues men from all these tragedies. This is part of the description of him:

> The new lord of the earth was, before all things, a tender-hearted philanthropist, and not only a philanthropist but a philosopher. He himself was a vegetarian. He forbad vivisection, and instituted a strict watch over slaughter-houses. The society for the protection of animals was encouraged by him in every way. But more important than all these details was the solid establishment among all mankind of the most fundamental equality, *an equality of general repletion*. This was accomplished in the second year of his reign. The social-political question was definitely settled, but if repletion be the first interest of hungry people, such people, when once replete, want something more. Even animals, when replete, usually want not only to sleep, but to play. Much more than they, do human beings, who at all times, *post panem*, have demanded *circenses*.

Then he goes on to describe how the equality of repletion is capped by some magic performances etcetera. Soloviev, *ex contrario*, argues the same way as Chesterton and the Book of Revelation: Repletion, comfort, is not really what we are here for, or what at the bottom of our souls we really desire.

We respond to this book even if we cannot expect to understand every little detail. And so perhaps it gradually becomes something that may mean more than a theoretical study; it can bring a personal message to us. Goethe said that the purpose of the study of history is that it awakens enthusiasm. I would like to vary this and say, in conclusion, that the purpose of the study of the Book of Revelation is that it awakens not only enthusiasm but also *devotion* and a *burning desire* to continue to work with the human race and to improve our planet until it takes the shape of the New Jerusalem.

The Crossing of the Threshold

It will be worth our while again, by way of introduction, to make a few general comments on the whole subject of the interpretation of scripture in general and the Apocalypse in particular. This was a subject in which earlier centuries were deeply involved, and passionately argued about, as we do today perhaps about Vietnam, socialism, devaluation, currency reform etcetera. A leading thinker, a church father living at the end of the second and beginning of the third century, Origen, developed a kind of comprehensive theory about it, which is still valuable. It is generally known as his doctrine of the threefold interpretation of scripture. He pointed out that, for a *full* interpretation of holy scripture, you needed to study first the *historical*, the physical part of it. We have done that in some measure in our lectures when we spoke of the seven churches of Asia, their historical background and situation and so forth. Secondly, the interpretation should concern itself with the *moral* implication, the moral teaching, of a particular piece of scripture. We have not done a great deal about that directly. We have not, for instance, dwelt much on the famous golden phrases in the messages to the churches: 'Be faithful unto death and I shall give you a crown of life', and things of that kind. It is not that we underestimate this aspect but that it is normally dealt with elsewhere; this is the province with which the traditional established churches mainly deal. Thirdly, however, he says that the full interpretation of scripture requires a third treatment, and that is the interpretation on the level of the *spirit*, what we should call, perhaps, the mystical, the esoteric, or the occult interpretation. On this platform, we must regard it as our specific contribution to deal with this level, with this particular aspect.

We can fairly easily find that the Book of Revelation *itself* suggests that interpretation. You may recall that in the very beginning we are told that this book descends from God to Christ, through the whole seven stages, down to those who receive it and ponder it. And we are told that it is set in pictures ('signified' is the word the Authorised Version uses) – it is set in symbols. If we anticipate a verse from the chapter with which we shall shortly be dealing, there is the reference to the two witnesses who are killed and whose bodies lie 'in the street of that great city which *spiritually* is called Sodom and Egypt, where also our Lord was crucified'. Now obviously, 'where our Lord was crucified' is Jerusalem (and incidentally this is the only reference in the whole book to the historical foundation of Christianity). But the Greek qualification is *pneumatikos*, '*called with a spiritual term*, Sodom and Egypt'. We may surmise that this phrase was used in the occult circles at the time because Jerusalem no longer deserved its original name, City of Peace, after the crucifixion of Christ, but showed more the character of the wickedness of Sodom and the tyranny of Egypt. I am offering this explanation for the two names, but the main point I want to make is that the

94

book *itself* makes such references that we have to understand it *pneumatikos*, in a spiritual fashion, in an esoteric, in an occult fashion. This is really the level on which we are now attempting to understand the book.

We are now moving in our studies towards a very important stage, which, in the title for tonight, has been described as 'The Crossing of the Threshold'. This is an important moment, an important stage, and the Apocalypse shares that quality which books of this kind have of combining a description or revelation of hidden events and causes of human evolution with an indication of the stages through which the human soul may pass on its pilgrimage to higher knowledge, on its path of initiation. It belongs to the character and skill and artistry of such books to merge these two things. Many of the things we have so far looked at and tried to understand as phases in the evolution of mankind, we can also look at as events, as experiences, as manifestations of spiritual reality, that a soul would encounter on its path of inward progress. From one angle, the pictures of the Book of Revelation are like a sequence of dramatic events, scenes of a sacred drama. But, if we allow them to penetrate, to shatter our souls, perhaps, so that they have that effect on us that Aristotle described in relation to the ancient tragic dramas – that they produce a *catharsis* in the human soul through awe and compassion, then we assimilate them as stages of our own development to the point of reaching the threshold leading from one level of experience into another.

Let me just illustrate that point in a little more detail. Last time we spoke of the haunting animal visions: the locusts, those monster horses with human faces and scorpion tails, and scorpions. We said that these are real astral visions and that there may easily be in the human race at certain times, at certain important moments of history, human beings who in their auras would appear like this. In that sense, this is an esoteric, historical reality. At the same time, we can apply this vision as a test to ourselves. Do we have such tendencies? Is there something in us that might one day manifest itself in this form and become a kind of challenge to ourselves, a spectre we have to face, to live with, and to overcome on the path of our own apocalyptic, personal progress?

There is one detail which I bypassed last time to which I want to go back before we come to the threshold, just to illustrate this approach in another way. I confine myself to reading a section of the twelfth verse of the eighth chapter, which is a kind of representative description of events that are described on several occasions, where it says that 'the third part of the sun was smitten, and the third part of the moon, and the third part of the stars; so as the third part of them was darkened, and the day shone not for a third part of it, and the night likewise'. What is meant by this description of a third part of the sun and the moon being darkened, and a third of the stars no longer shining, or, as we find in the twelfth chapter, falling to the earth? Are these to be cosmic catastrophes in the material sense as some artists have painted them? Or are we dealing with something quite different? Our relationship to, and to some extent perhaps our dependence on, the world of sun and moon and stars is far greater than we are normally aware. We all enjoy, of course, the light of the sun; we wait impatiently for the days to get longer and the sun to get stronger. We love the light of the moon, we admire the brilliance of a starry sky, but even in the purely *physical* sphere we have, within the last hundred years or so, gone beyond the immediate field of observation; we have extended the spectrum; we now speak of ultra-violet rays, of infra-red rays, rays which our eyes cannot immediately observe. We also become aware of other radiations of a kind, but, in order to understand what the Apocalypse speaks about, we have to extend our understanding of these influences beyond the range of physical observation. It is quite obvious to us, although we do not understand the mysterious details, that the rays of the sun have something to do with life, that the whole world of the plants depends on them, and, in some more mysterious, subtle way even, on the influences of the moon. We are not, however, in a position, we have not the instruments today, to *test* these radiations, these influences, really adequately. In fact, we are far worse off in this field of study than earlier centuries were.

As far as I know, Rudolf Steiner made no reference to the particular passage we are discussing, but he gave a most interesting clue to the understanding of this whole world of subtle influences. He did so in connection with a visit to this country. During the years 1922, 1923 and 1924, he came on visits to this country, and in 1923 there was a summer school held in North Wales at Penmaenmawr. Rudolf Steiner was led to the remnants of the two Druid Circles which you find there. There are, of course, better examples in the country, let alone Stonehenge, but this was the situation and he gave his great interest, his searching mind to these, let us call them, Druid remains.

Soon afterwards he spoke about the principle of the Druid religion and the whole Druid civilisation. He said that what they were really interested in was the *shadow*. All their megalithic arrangements were designed to enable them to study the shadow, not the physical light. Take, for instance, the simplest of these megalithic constructions, the dolmen: a few boulders arranged in a rough circle, with a very vast boulder on top, which, incidentally, had to be of igneous rock, silica formation, granite. The physical sunlight would stream down from the sky on to this natural chapel, but *through* the boulder would penetrate the suprasensory sunlight, the non-physical, the spiritual radiations. After meditative preparation, the Druid priest would sit in the shadow, which was charged with the spiritual radiations of the sunlight, and inspired by this content of the shadow, he would learn the great secrets about man and the universe; he would contact the cosmic memory, and he would also be able to direct and instruct his people in the daily routine, seed time and harvest, and the other social and economic necessities of the day.

Now it is this field of influences (which is so remote from our normal observation today) with which we must deal, or which at least we must include, if we read such passages in the Book of Revelation. We need not even go into that kind of starry influence with which astrology deals; we can confine ourselves entirely to these matters of which I have spoken. But those who can penetrate with their investigation into this field, as Rudolf Steiner himself was able to do, would report to us that indeed a great proportion of what was once a spiritual gift that came to man by

98

means of the sun's rays, *is no longer coming*; that the spiritual nourishment that sun, moon and stars gave to the human race, real *life* rays (we talk about death-rays and are interested in them) are no longer operating to the same degree; they are vanishing, they *have vanished*. The Book of Revelation speaks of such realities as part of that progress of humanity with which it deals, speaks of it as part of the hidden background to human history, which, as you remember, I said Steiner says we only dream. We *dream* all these things, and it needs an awakened consciousness like Steiner's occasionally to tell us what we really do dream. We dream this real fact that a third of what humanity used to receive from the heavens in the light, in the radiations, is no longer coming but is fallen to the earth.

The book itself does not say what we can do with this situation, but this is somewhat in keeping with the whole style of the book, that it can speak more of the necessity of doom than the freedom of redemption, because the necessity of doom, the consequences of what happened at the beginning, are calculable; what happens in freedom, what man does with these things, cannot really be predicted because freedom is unpredictable. Only a door can be left open for it. Steiner himself, however, has gone further than this, and his description of this becoming silent of the heavens, man's noticing it and feeling the loss and the deprivation, half consciously, perhaps, in his lack of pure natural vitality, is amongst some of the most wonderful things of which he spoke. He says that the opposite can come about. There may be men sufficiently active, sufficiently mature and advanced, to give *back* some of the rays which once upon a time the cosmos gave to man. He put this observation into a few simple lines which he wrote down as a Christmas message to Frau Marie Steiner at Christmas, 1922. These are the lines, first in German and then in English translation, summing up the matter which I have very briefly tried to put before you.

Sterne sprachen einst zu Menschen,
Ihr Verstummen ist Weltenschicksal;
Des Verstummens Wahrnehmung
Kann Leid sein des Erdenmenschen;
In der stummen Stille aber reift
Was Menschen sprechen zu Sternen;
Ihres Sprechens Wahrnehmung
Kann Kraft werden des Geistesmenschen.

The stars spake once to man.
It is world destiny that they are silent now.
To be aware of the silence
Can become pain for earthly man;
But, in the deepening silence, grows and ripens
What man speaks to the stars;
To be aware of the speaking
Can become strength to spirit-man.

* * *

We now come to the tenth chapter, which seems to mark the crossing of a threshold. There descends a mighty angel, whom one would expect to find at this place, a figure whom we may call the Guardian of the Threshold. He is described as a mighty angel, with a voice as powerful as a lion; his countenance shines like the sun; he has a cloud about him, a rainbow on his head, and his feet are of fire. We are told that he set his right foot upon the sea and his left foot upon the earth. They form a gate.

At the same time this describes the step we are now taking, from the firm land of the earth on to the water. This is an experience of which you can speak comparatively early in your travels in this world, when you tentatively come to the shore where the accustomed firm land of logical thought, deduction, conclusion and argument with which we live and on which we rely, suddenly becomes no longer really so useful, where you have to leave it behind, where you enter into another field of observation and experience, where you really enter into what Rudolf Steiner once called 'the Ocean-Being of the Spirit'. The moment you go into this world, leaving the reliable firm ground of your consciousness behind, there is always the sensation that you move into a watery, into an unstable world; you walk on the sea and begin to fear that you may drown. It is a very distinctive feature of that threshold: one foot on the earth, one foot on the water.

This figure speaks with a loud voice – a challenge; and then we are told that when he had cried out, 'seven thunders uttered their voices. And when the seven thunders had uttered their voices, I was about to write: and I heard a voice from heaven saying unto me, Seal up those things which the seven thunders uttered, and write them not.' There is a cosmic dialogue between the Guardian and the seven thunders, and that is a secret, a mystery, that must not yet, at any rate, be revealed.

The angel appears at the same time as the genius of man, as the greatest semblance, the image, into which the disciple on the path now wants to grow. The three different functions of his soul are pictorially expressed: his thinking quality in the cloud realm, his feeling quality in the whole range of the colours of the rainbow, his will forces in the fiery feet with which he walks. But this threefold manifestation of his being is held together by the countenance which shines like a sun, in which the higher self, the spiritual ego, rests, and, in a sense, is enthroned.

Now this Guardian raises his hand and makes a tremendous declaration: that there shall be no more time. Again, a typical characteristic, because we are told that when we cross the threshold *time* becomes *space*. There is a famous reference to this in Wagner's *Parsifal,* when Parsifal first comes to the castle of the Grail. He speaks to old Gurnemanz, who leads him:

> Ich schreite kaum, –
> doch wähn' ich mich schon weit.

Gurnemanz replies:

> Du siehst, mein Sohn,
> zum Raum wird hier die Zeit.

> I hardly move,
> yet deem myself now far.

And Gurnemanz:

> Thou seest, my son,
> To space time changes here.

And this is what the angel says. There shall be time no longer; we enter into space at this point.

Then comes the final action at this threshold, which we have quoted once or twice out of this particular context because it is so important in a general way. He takes the book, the scroll, and tells John, who is now the one who crosses the threshold, to *eat* it, to *swallow* it. This represents the kind of internal transformation: you are no longer to read, to look from outside, even with spiritual eyes, but take it right into yourself; it is sweet on your tongue, but makes your belly bitter. It transforms you, it sets up a tremendous revolution in you; this crossing of the threshold turns you inside out, one might say. It is something which takes the *whole* human being into the process.

The angel of the threshold has already prepared us for what follows:

> But in the days of the voice of the seventh angel, when he shall begin to sound, the mystery of God should be finished, as he has declared to his servants the prophets.

Once we are in the sphere of the seventh trumpet, in a sense we remain there to the end because everything happens from now onwards within that sphere. Scholars have said that the seventh trumpet is the apocalypse within the Apocalypse, which is just a way of saying that there is a kernel within the nut.

'When he shall begin to sound, the mystery of God should be finished' – When is this? No doubt those of you who have tried to understand the Apocalypse will confirm my experience that you do not really get into the book simply by burning midnight oil. There comes an end; but then there come moments when suddenly things light up. A few weeks ago, I was taking part in a weekend on the Apocalypse in a college in the west of England, and in the question time somebody asked me just that question: When does the seventh trumpet sound? On the spur of the moment, I answered: 'It sounds all the time. It only depends on who can hear it'. And I think perhaps this is the answer. The seventh trumpet sounds all the time or, in other words, the mysterious purposes of God are being fulfilled all the time, but far, far from the forefront of our everyday life. We should have to rise into those levels to know it, but there, in a sense, it sounds all the time, and in that sense also, time becomes space. It is always there, and at the same time, of course, it rolls on in that sort of space-time in which we live with our consciousness.

Before we come to what is really the heart piece of the book (Chapter 12), we are bothered, in a sense (I can only say 'bothered'), with the eleventh chapter, in which there is the story of the two witnesses and their tragic fate. They are not named, but they are described in such a way that we can surmise who they are. They 'have power to shut heaven that it rain not . . . and have power over waters to turn them to blood, and to smite the earth with all plagues, as often as they will'. Quite obviously, the first one, who has power 'to shut heaven that it rain not' is Elijah, who is introduced in the First Book of Kings as Elijah the Tishbite, who tells King Ahab that 'there shall not be dew nor rain these years but according to my word'. The other, who turns water into blood and can bring plagues, is obviously Moses. They are the two figures also described as appearing at the scene of the Transfiguration, representative of the Law and the Prophets. But if we say the Law and the Prophets we confine the image only to the Old Testament tradition. In a very much wider sense, the one is the law-giver, the man who gives order; the other is the prophet, the one who breaks into the future. If I may use the terms – we have the 'conservative' law-giver and the 'radical' prophet: the two principles of human order and evolution – conservatism and radicalism, represented in their spiritual form. Because these two principles are obviously part of all life, all history, of all development, they are *built* in the order of our existence; and in their highest form they are shown in these two great characters: Moses, the law-giver, and Elijah, the prophet. They were built into the Temple of Solomon as the two famous pillars: the Pillar of Wisdom and the Pillar of Strength. Strange things, however, follow. They are killed and their bodies lie exposed in the city 'which spiritually is called Sodom and Egypt, where our Lord was crucified'. And then after three and a half days (note the significant time) the spirit of life is breathed into them and they are taken into heaven.

I will not offer a close explanation – I am not able to do so – but we might remember that it seems to be a subject which has haunted writers and artists through the ages. One of the earliest preserved fragments of poetry in the German language, in what is known as Old High German, deals with it, and mentions Elijah by name.* Whether it was only the passage in the Apocalypse or some deeper link with this subject that made this unknown poet write the poem, I do not know, but we have a similar reference to it in Soloviev's story of the Antichrist; in fact that is how he finishes his story.

The two representatives, the two witnesses, in his story are the leader of the western church, Pope Peter, and the leader of the eastern church, John. One might say: the man of order in the west and the man of

* *Muspilli* of the ninth century.

105

prophecy in the east. In their great meeting with the universal Emperor, who is the benevolent Antichrist, they are killed and lie exposed in the streets of Jerusalem. The small band of real Christians who escaped to the heights of Jericho are now under the leadership of Professor Pauli, the German theologian, who is the third of the witnesses, and, though of minor importance, he is given the honour of leading the faithful remnant.

On the evening of the fourth day as it became dark, Professor Pauli and ten companions, mounted on asses and taking with them a cart, stole into Jerusalem and through side streets, past Kharam-esh-Sherif, came out on Kharet-en-Nasar and approached the entrance to the Church of the Resurrection, where on the pavement lay the bodies of Pope Peter and the venerable John. The street at this hour was empty, every-body had gone to Kharam-esh-Sherif. The soldiers on guard had fallen into a deep sleep. Those who came for the bodies found them entirely untouched by corruption, and not even stiff or heavy. Having raised them upon the stretchers and having covered them with the mantles they had brought, they returned by the same roundabout way to their own people, but scarcely had they lowered the stretchers on the ground than the spirit of life entered into the dead. They moved and attempted to throw off the cloaks in which they were wrapped. All with joyful cries began to assist them, and both having come to life, stood up on their feet, whole and sound. And the venerable John began to speak: 'So, little children, we have not parted, and now I say to you, it is time to carry out Christ's last prayer about his followers, that they should be one even as He with the Father is one . . .'

A little further on we read:

The darkness was suddenly lightened by a bright splendour and there appeared a great wonder in heaven: a woman clothed in the sun with the moon under her feet and a crown of twelve stars on her head. The apparition remained for some time in one place and then moved slowly towards the south. Pope Peter raised his staff and cried out: 'There is our banner, let us follow it'.

That is a metamorphosis of this story, and the banner will be our main subject next time. It is the heart piece of the book, but as I have to rearrange my remaining material from four into three lectures, I will try your patience for a little longer and go straight on to Chapter 13 and, as my last section, speak briefly about the beast.

* * *

Another of the haunting pictures of the book is the beast with the seven heads and ten horns. We read at the beginning of the thirteenth chapter:

And I stood upon the sand of the sea, and saw a beast rise up out of the sea, having seven heads and ten horns, and upon his horns ten crowns, and upon his heads the name of blasphemy ... And he opened his mouth in blasphemy against God, to blaspheme his name, and his tabernacle, and them that dwell in heaven.

Through the tapestries of Bayeux from the Middle Ages, through the great altar-piece in the Victoria and Albert Museum, and the many presentations of the Apocalypse in Byzantine art, this picture of the beast with the seven heads and the ten horns rising out of the sea is always treated with a kind of special attention. In his lectures, Rudolf Steiner speaks of the occult terminology that is used here, and that is not very easy to understand. He says that if an occult document speaks of *head* in that context, it is something that is formed in the etheric realm, in the etheric body, the sphere of life. When it is projected into the *physical*, then it is called a horn. I have tried to understand it for myself by using quite modern medical language where one speaks of a functional disease and an organic disease. A functional disease still remains in the etheric: you can have a functional disease of the kidneys, owing perhaps to some kind of emotional, psychological, disturbance; and then, of course, the functional disease can become a real disease of the organ, or an organic disease, which you can trace. Now, if I understand rightly what Steiner says, the functional disease would be a head, the organic disease a horn.

For me, the most immediately helpful light thrown on this picture which I have encountered came from a medical friend. He was a doctor who really also looked upon the human body not only in its material and purely physiological manifestations but as an apocalyptic document, if you like, because our body is in itself full of apocalyptic significance if we could but read it. He tried to read the system of the endocrine secretions in terms of the beast with the seven heads and the ten horns. We have seven ductless glands: epiphysis, hypophysis, thyroid, the parathyroids, pancreas, the adrenals and gonads. Some of them are physically so minute, like the parathyroid, that they are really almost only functions. The whole system is largely a functional system; we depend on its proper function enormously, and the slightest disturbance of it shows itself in quite far-reaching results. There are three pairs amongst these glands, there being two parathyroids, two adrenals and two gonads, so in their *physical* expression they have ten 'horns'. It has a fascinating appeal, the thought of the endocrinal system with its seven heads and ten horns as a beast which lives in us and rises out of the sea – for it lives in our juices, in our liquids, whilst itself, of course, secreting liquid. In its total function as a system, of course, it keeps us very much on the animal level. It is our task as human beings to control it. Fortunately, at this stage of evolution, unless it goes wrong, we know very little about it, we take it for granted. On the other hand, I remember that after this whole system was first properly studied at the beginning of the century, it became a sort of popular knowledge in the twenties and thirties, and you could easily hear at that time this announcement: 'Well I can't do anything about it – it's my glands.' One felt so much bound by this.

This morning I read in *The Guardian* a report on a congress of biologists for which the paper gave the headline: 'The Atom Bomb of the Biologists'. Apparently the research work of a number of years was concentrated and reported upon, and it had to do with genetics. It really faced the problem: are we coming near the point where, through work in the laboratory, we can gradually influence hereditary qualities, influence right from the beginning the developing human germ? According to the report, we have not quite reached that stage yet, but we have made steps in that direction. And very rightly the congress raised the question: 'Who will set the standard?' Supposing we *can* produce chromosomes of a certain kind and find ways and means of injecting them into the earliest stages of the human germ, who sets the standards? Will there be an infallible man in the world, will there be a committee, will there be an international committee? You can see the whole night-mare of the idea. This is the sphere of the beast. If for a moment we adopt my medical friend's suggestion, certainly, among other things, this system in us is a kind of apocalyptic projection into our own physiological make-up. It is in this sphere where microbiology would operate, and where, in a sense, some of these apocalyptic spectres leave the book and begin to stalk abroad. So this is by no means only a fascinating vision which the artist can paint, but it is a picture which can come very closely home.

Rudolf Steiner speaks quite specifically about this beast, about its being potentially there in all of us as something to live with, to work with, to transform and to conquer. But, his gaze goes far ahead in evolution to the point when a division in the human race will become inevitable and all this will come to its fulfil-ment at the time when our whole earth, our whole solar system, moves into another form of existence, passes through a spiritual state and then enters into a new form of manifestation. He looks ahead to the far distant moment when that kind of division and decision will take place. This is what he says at the end of his tenth lecture:

Man has the seven heads and ten horns within him. He must now work upon these through the reception of the Christ-principle so that they shall be destroyed, so to speak. For each time a man dies, the seven-headed and ten-horned nature can clearly be seen in his astral body. This is merely held together like a piece of indiarubber which has been correspondingly formed. Now suppose a person hardened himself during our epoch against the Christ-principle and were to come to the time of the great War of All against All without having had the Christ-experience, suppose he were to come to this time and had thrust the Christ away from him, then when the earth passes over into the astral, whatever was there and which he ought to have changed, would spring forth, it would spring forth in its old form. The beast with the seven heads and the ten horns would appear, whereas in those who have received the Christ-principle, sexuality will again be overcome. The hardened ones will . . . appear in their totality as the beast with seven heads and ten horns . . . They can be transformed through the reception of the Christ-impulse, but if Christ is rejected they will remain and they will reappear in the period indicated by the falling of the vials of wrath and the earth splitting, as it were, into two parts, one in which the Christ-men appear with white garments as the elect, . . . and the other part in which men appear in the form of the beast with seven heads and ten horns.

Now fortunately, and in a sense as a matter of comfort, Steiner says these final divisions are far, far ahead in time, but we are moving towards them, and even now we can select our direction because, as we shall see in the last two lectures, he has helped us to understand that this division of which he speaks makes its appearance felt first in this century.

The War in Heaven – The Double Face of Evil – The Beast and its Number

> But in the days of the voice of the seventh angel, when he shall begin to sound, the mysterious purposes of God shall be brought to fulfilment, as he has proclaimed to his servants the prophets.

That is the promise of the seventh trumpet, and a little later we read that the seventh angel actually sounded his trumpet.

We said last time that the seventh angel really sounds all the time and that it depends on us, on the *degree* of our inner awareness, as to whether we can hear his sound or not. It is therefore an interesting question to ask: What can we do so as to be able to tune in to those sounds, to tune in, to use a phrase of Rudolf Steiner's, to the *Posaunen Sprache der Erzengel*, to tune in to 'the trumpet idiom of the archangels'. Of course, if you use such a phrase in the present intellectual climate of civilisation, people think that you have perhaps taken leave of your senses. How can anybody in his senses talk about 'the trumpet idiom of the archangels'? This is begging the question. Do we really always *want* to stay in our senses? Perhaps the whole anthroposophical endeavour is directed towards taking *leave* of our senses, to transcending the limitation of our normal sense world, to being transcendental. Rudolf Steiner in his own quite rational, conscious and scientific way explained how the human soul is really capable of tuning in to this trumpet idiom of the archangels.

He acknowledges, of course, that our ordinary day-mind with its normal intellectual operations cannot immediately make any contact with that sphere; but we also have a night-mind, and, as he so often describes, during the night soul and spirit are disengaged from their normal absorption in the bodily framework and take leave of the senses, but pay for that leave by unconsciousness. On the other hand, he himself, by means of advanced development in the spiritual sphere, reached that stage where the whole range of the experience of the night-mind became an object of research and understanding to him. Towards the last few years of his life he studied this field and came to certain conclusions about the relationship of man's soul to the trumpet idiom of the archangels. He simply said that those human souls who during the day introduce some kind of spiritual interest, spiritual content into their human relationships, and in particular into their conversations, are carried at night into that sphere. Then in the deeper layers of their consciousness, in the subconscious, they carry across something of that contact with the idiom of the archangels into daily life.

He was particularly occupied with these problems in 1923 and as his wife, Marie Steiner, was away on a tour with the eurythmy group for a considerable time, he summed up some of these matters in a concise manner in one of his letters to her, which were published last year in commemoration of the centenary of her birth. It is particularly appropriate tonight to draw

113

one or two quotations from that more intimate sphere because today is the anniversary of Steiner's own birthday. This is what he wrote:

> At the present time man needs a fresh spiritual content for the words he speaks because soul and spirit, when outside the body in sleep, retain of the spoken word only what refers to the spiritual. For man needs to reach out in his sleep as far as the realm of the archangeloi for an understanding and conversation with them; and they receive only the spiritual content, never the material content, of our words. Failing such content and understanding, man suffers harm in his whole being.

Thus he describes in what a comparatively simple way such a contact is possible, but adds the caution that unless such contacts are made we may even suffer harm in our own being. Why this is so I suppose will become apparent as we proceed. We do so, assuming that we would not be here if we were not people who at least at times carry some spiritual content into our conversations, who are therefore somewhat prepared, if only through sleep, for the messages that come from that sphere and are contained in the Book of Revelation.

*   *   *

We now continue to read two verses from the eleventh chapter and then the greater part of the twelfth chapter. I omit, only for the sake of economy, what in a musical composition might be described as transitional bars.

> And the seventh angel sounded; and there were great voices in heaven, saying, The kingdoms of this world are become the kingdoms of our Lord, and of his Christ; and he shall reign for ever and ever ... And the temple of God was

opened in heaven, and there was seen in his temple the ark of his testament; and there were lightnings, and voices, and thunderings, and an earthquake, and great hail.

Tremendous cosmic commotion goes together with the sound of the seventh trumpet. And now follows the main content of that revelation in the twelfth chapter, which is both mathematically the centre, and qualitatively the heartpiece of the book. It takes in the Book of Revelation the place that the eleventh chapter, recording the Raising of Lazarus, takes in the Gospel of St. John.

And there appeared a great wonder in heaven; a woman clothed with the sun, and the moon under her feet, and upon her head a crown of twelve stars. And she being with child, cried travailing in birth, and pained to be delivered. And there appeared another wonder in heaven; and behold a great red dragon, having seven heads and ten horns and seven crowns upon his heads. And his tail drew the third part of the stars of heaven, and did cast them to the earth: and the dragon stood before the woman which was ready to be delivered, for to devour her child as soon as it was born. And she brought forth a man child, who was to rule all nations with a rod of iron: and her child was caught up unto God, and to his throne. And the woman fled into the wilderness, where she hath a place prepared of God, that they should feed her there a thousand two hundred and three-score days. And there was war in heaven: Michael and his angels fought against the dragon; and the dragon fought and his angels, and prevailed not; neither was their place found any more in heaven. And the great dragon was cast out, that old serpent, called the Devil, and Satan, which deceiveth the whole world: he was cast out into the earth, and his angels were cast out with him . . . And when the dragon saw that he was cast unto the earth, he persecuted the woman which brought forth the man child. And to the woman were given two wings of a great eagle, that she might fly into the wilderness, into her place, where she is nourished for a time, and times, and half a time, from the face of the serpent. And the serpent cast out of his mouth water as a flood after the woman, that he might cause her to be carried away of the flood. And the earth helped the woman, and the earth opened her mouth, and swallowed up the flood which the dragon cast out of his mouth.

That is the substance of the twelfth chapter and the message of the seventh trumpet. On the face of it, perhaps, it does not even strike us as being of enormous significance, so we have to dig a little more deeply. The book begins by calling it a 'wonder'. It is rather remarkable; the Greek *semeion* is usually translated in the Authorised Version of the New Testament as either 'miracle' or 'sign', never as 'wonder', except just here. There are two wonders: the woman clothed with the sun, and then the dragon.

I believe it is not difficult, even for anyone who is not really familiar with the apocalyptic way of writing, to see in that woman, man's soul; and those a little familiar with occult cosmology can see that in the way in which she is described we are reminded of the three phases of planetary evolution of the earth: the Saturn phase, represented by the circle of stars on her head; the Sun phase by the cloak around her shoulders; the Moon phase by the moon under her feet, the immediate planetary past on which her feet rest; and then her story is concentrated upon the main significance of the present Earth phase of our cosmos, in which the soul of man is to bring forth a child, a self, a spiritual individuality, an ego. The whole dynamic tension of the picture is to start with concentrated on that event: the woman is going to give birth to a child. And this child is specifically described as a *male* child – the male principle, you might almost say, *the* masculine. This child is to rule the nations with a rod of iron. The Greek has a wonderful phrase for that iron rod: *rabdos sidera*. I would like to translate it: 'a wand of starry steel'. And the Greek used for the activity of the child is *poimainein*, 'to shepherd'. That male being should shepherd humanity with a wand, with a shepherd's crook of star-made steel; that is his function.

But the birth is contended. There is the dragon lying in wait, and 'dragon' itself is a word with a great deal of history to it. I do not want to go too far into purely etymological studies, but they are sometimes very helpful. 'Dragon' comes from a word which is used in Greek poetry, and poetry only, meaning really 'to see', 'to look', 'to have a piercing look at things'. That is the chief quality of the dragon: he looks at you with a piercing look. If it was said in the first chapter that the Son of Man, the human form divine, has eyes like flaming fire, then the dragon has eyes like fireworks. He is fiery red – *pyrros* in the Greek, which really means red, but red derived from fire. There he lies in wait to devour the child when it is born, to eat it up and make use of it for his own purposes.

In between his persecution of the woman comes his fight with Michael, about which I will speak presently, when he is overthrown. Then in his defeat he yields up some of his deeper secret, for then he is described as 'that old serpent, called the Devil and Satan'. 'That old serpent' is almost a bit too pleasant and too familiar. *Ophis ho archaios* is the archetypal, the primeval serpent, the Ur-serpent, the origin and pattern of anything serpent-like. Here, and here only, in the New

Testament, the dual nature of evil is put into words: Devil and Satan. The anthroposophical terms, in Steiner's tradition and teaching, are Lucifer and Ahriman. One can hardly just pass this over without for a moment dwelling on this *fundamental* conception in Steiner's teaching that the ethical conflict does not consist of a simple antithesis between good and evil, between light and darkness, but that a good always comes about as a creative act which strikes a proper balance between the too much and the too little, between the too hot and the too cold, between the too high and the too low, too soft and too hard, between two extremes: the red Devil, Lucifer, and the black Satan, Ahriman; between the devil of the red-hot passion, Lucifer, and the devil of the ice-cold cynicism, Ahriman. And here for once, in this defeat when he is thrown down to earth (not in heaven, but the moment he is thrown down to earth) he yields the double nature of evil, the double name, Lucifer and Ahriman, Devil and Satan.

To return to the woman and her strange story: her child is caught up to God, and to His throne. She flees into the wilderness, and we may remember from previous studies that the Greek word for 'wilderness' is always identical with 'loneliness'. It is the word from which 'hermit' is derived, one who goes into the loneliness of the desert. She is removed into loneliness (*eremon*), but in her loneliness she is protected for 1,260 days. Here we come to numerology again, a code number to disguise the critical three and a half. The year in the old days was divided into 360 days: 1,260 days, therefore, is three and a half years, (3 x 360 plus 180), and there we have the critical figure of three and a half that always indicates a significant period of time, one that has a dynamic quality of beginning, climax and descent; it numbers the days of initiation in the ancient mysteries and a little later on in the same chapter, as you may remember, it appears as 'a time, and times and half a time'. The mysterious, critical three and a half is always disguised. The woman, then, is given a place; there she can rest, but in loneliness, whilst her son, the male principle, the spiritual ego, is removed, is caught up to God and His throne.

Here, in apocalyptic idiom, we touch on a great fundamental problem of our spiritual existence with which in many ways we are battling today very, very severely, and which again I should like to introduce from Rudolf Steiner's own studies. He draws on apocalyptic passages outside the Book of Revelation, in particular on the Pauline epistles. There is a passage in the third chapter of the Epistle to the Colossians that he translated in a particular way and used as a background to speak on this profound matter. In the Authorised Version the verses read: 'For ye are dead, and your life is hid with Christ in God. When Christ, who is our life, shall appear, then shall ye also appear with him in glory.' In his translation (in turn translated into English), it would read like this: 'You are dead and your ego is hidden with Christ in the spiritual world. But when Christ Himself, who carries our ego, will make Himself seen again, you, too, will manifest yourselves with Him.'

We are dead – in other words we are not really here at all, but our *true* self is hidden in the spiritual world with Christ, as Paul says. But, if the Christ makes

Himself visible again, if there is a new *parousia*, then we shall be drawn into this, and we shall also appear in glory, appear with our true self. Normally, of course, we think we *do* have an ego; we say all the time: *I* do so and so, *I* see, *I* will etcetera; but, strictly speaking, this is (as certain schools of contemporary psychology would also assert) nothing but a *mirror* ego. It is, in Steiner's terms, an ego-consciousness, it is a reflection of the real thing, and of the real thing we know nothing, generally speaking.

The real thing, for instance, is the organiser and operator of our destiny; and we know how *alien* we feel the force that brings about our destiny – but that is our *real spiritual self*. We feel it as if it were a force coming from outside because we are not yet conscious in this realm; we know only a reflection. Somewhat earlier on, Rudolf Steiner dwelt on this matter and brought the results of this particular research into two books, which he published during the First World War: *Vom Menschenrätsel* and *Von Seelenrätseln*, (*Riddles of Man* and *Riddles of the Soul*). He also gave a short summary in a letter to his wife, which I will read because it illumines this particular fundamental problem very simply.

> It is a breath taken from the world of spirit, the real self, which in the ebb and flow of existence streams through to the body when we are awake, and flows from the body when we go to sleep. In this breathing of the spirit, I am but like the air in the lung – not lung am I. No. Air, breath. The lung is that which knows of me. If I grasp this truth, I recognise myself in the spirit of the world.

It is a difficult conception, but a very true and very real one with which, I believe, we touch an extraordinarily intimate problem concerning the souls and spiritual life of human beings today.

At the time when the first electronic brain was constructed in 1948 (which you can now see exhibited in a shop in New York), Professor Wiener of the Massachusetts Institute of Technology produced some fundamental studies of the human brain and nervous system in which he tried, on the basis of the experience of constructing an electronic brain, to describe the whole functioning of our brain and nerves, our whole sensory organism, in terms of atomic physics, in terms of radiations, minute but quite measurable stimuli from brain cell to brain cell – the whole human being in a kind of state of fission, whereby the cells are activated and produce consciousness. These studies have been carried very far. Some of you may listen to talks on the radio or, if not, read them in *The Listener*. In the last few weeks quite startling accounts have been given of how attempts are being made to describe the whole consciousness of man in these terms. There is still, however, one problem, and from the point of view of anthroposophical epistemology, it is an interesting one: they say there is always a 'plus' in the brain – to use anthroposophical phrases, the concept is always greater than the sum total of the percepts or the sense-data. Where does this what they call 'soft-ware programme' of the brain come from? When that problem is solved, more can be done. I will read the last two sentences of the last talk:

> The challenge now is to discover the soft-ware programmes used by the brain, to read reality from the fleeting cartoon picture in the eyes.

(Our ordinary sense perceptions are described as 'fleeting cartoon pictures', but we read reality from these fleeting cartoon pictures because there is a 'soft-ware programme' in our brain.)

We will then build machines that can see.

Possibly we shall. Personally, I have no doubt that this is quite true, but, viewing this with detachment, without fanaticism, one is led to ask a question (and you will presently see that this is really all relevant to our picture) which the atomic scientist does not seem to put. In *matter*, atomic radiation is a sign of distintegration, of ageing. Perhaps it is true that as the universe runs down, humanity also runs down, and we have these electric impulses resulting from nuclear fission as a gradual decadence in us. The question is: Has it always been so? And has the rate been constant? Once you probe that question you may come to the conclusion that it is by no means clear that it has always been constant, and that it is quite possible to think that this 'computerisation' of our organism is a comparatively recent development, part of the evolutionary stage at which we have arrived. It is even conceivable that, without wanting to do so, we promote it all the time. Rudolf Steiner once drew our attention to one particular difference between our age (that was fifty years ago) and the time of Goethe. He said that, as we all knew, the human body was a conductor of electricity; the air in our time, unlike Goethe's, was full of radiations and currents for which we were conductors. Fifty years ago that was nothing compared with the case *now*. Inductive electricity is constantly produced within us, particularly during the night; when we wake up in the morning our body is charged with inductive electricity. We may well ask if this is perhaps, without our wanting it or even knowing it, an influence that produces, that enhances and speeds up what I call this 'computerisation' of our organism?

These are very relevant questions. But are we now just the defenceless victims of evolution, evolution which to some extent we seem even ourselves to speed on the downward path? Is there only, to use the phrase from one of the previous talks, the necessity of doom, or are there areas of freedom, pockets of resistance, islands of redemption? You will expect Steiner to answer in the affirmative. In terms of this apocalyptic chapter he would draw our attention to the message of the book itself: that the dragon is overthrown, conquered, that while the child is still with God, yet the dragon is conquered. And the great conqueror is the Archangel Michael – his name is once used in this chapter. It is worth while remembering what that name means. It is a challenge. The names of the other archangels mean statements: Raphael, God Healer; Gabriel, God Strength – but Michael, Who like God? It is a challenging question. The old legends say it was the challenge he shouted across the world when Lucifer tried to usurp the throne of God. 'Who like God?' was his battle cry.

Perhaps today the answer to that question is a different one: Man. He was created in the image of God and the time is approaching when that promise should be and may be redeemed. It is with that background that Steiner's work and research really enter into this problem, first of all of recognising that our ego normally referred to is a mirror picture; on the other hand of feeling that the time has come, or is about to come, when the child returns from the throne of God. It is one of the deep psychological tensions of our time. In the last lecture we shall see another picture: the riders on the white horses, the transformed centaurs, riding into human beings. They are the final conquering ego, but they have to ride down a very great deal in us before they take possession, and that is the problem.

Today, quite a new term has been created for a particular psychotic condition – *autism*. We speak of the autistic human being, and, particularly, the autistic child, who is entirely concentrated and confined in his own interests. I am told the number of autistic children is fast increasing. What is the problem? Are they the first specimens of a human wave that is completely, finally computerised? Or are they, on the other hand, children in whom the real ego begins to assert itself, but with such overwhelming indwelling force that for the moment it is impossible for them to make contact or communicate? Perhaps we can see that on a vast national level this whole problem of the computer system and the sense of acquiring a true ego showed itself in what one might only call the national schizophrenia of Germany under the Nazis. On the face of it, it was a political problem; deeper down, of course, it was a profound human problem, and it was not by chance that it should have happened in Germany. Reading world history against the background of Steiner's work, one is led to think that this is the particular nation in which the ego problems predominate. It is an interesting fact that German is the only

European language that has its own name for the ego, used as a noun: *Das Ich*. We have to borrow the Latin 'ego'; to say 'the I' is artificial. The French cannot say it, nor the Russians, nor the Italians, the Scandinavians only up to a point. *Das Ich* is unique, and there has developed the Ich philosophy, starting with Fichte, with whom Steiner started himself, then a less known philosopher, Stirner, and then Nietzsche. As for Steiner himself, his philosophic work is an attempt to establish the true indwelling self, the child returning from the throne of God. Before his voice could be heard, however, this fantastic experiment of National Socialism was made, an attempt to find an ego through the development of hatred and the projection of all one's worst qualities on to a scapegoat. The problem is known also in other countries. Further, some of you may have read an article by David Holbrook in *The Guardian* last week where these matters were touched on, and where he referred to this particular problem as experienced, for instance, by Dylan Thomas in rather a different way. He says that Dylan Thomas, partly through alcoholism, lived a life of one stage after another of attempted self-destruction, in *order* to achieve a new birth. That is one way of trying to get the true ego through, as his last words, which Holbrook quotes, are aware: 'I wish I could be for ever unconscious. I want to go to the Garden of Eden.' (The child back to God's throne.) But, as Holbrook very rightly says, humanity *began* at Eden; we cannot go back. There can be no infantile regression, no going back into the womb and sleeping for ever; we can only go forward.

In the last year of his life, Rudolf Steiner concentrated his spiritual attention on a discovery of the true nature of the Archangel Michael, who for him became increasingly a tremendously real presence. It is very moving to see how in the last nine months of his active life, in 1924, he came back to it in nearly every lecture. Then, during the last six months when he was bed-ridden and wrote a message every week to the members of the movement, published in a special news sheet, in nearly every letter Michael is mentioned, each time described from a different angle as the great spiritual presence, who now, after the dragon has been cast down, helps 'the child' to return; who helps the soul, helps the woman to return after her 'time and times and half a time' from the wilderness to her proper place, from her loneliness to her proper existence.

So this apocalyptic heart-piece really speaks to the hidden background of our immediate time, of our present century. We can deepen its effect still further if we now risk proceeding beyond that chapter for a brief look into the next, which we partly already dealt with last time.

The next chapter opens with a description of the beast with seven heads and ten horns we spoke about last time, which rises from the sea. '. . . and power was given to him to continue forty and two months' (again that is three and a half: 3 x 12 plus 6). The sentence to which I should first like to draw attention is the following: 'The dragon gave him *his* power, and *his* seat, and great authority.' The beast rising from the abyss, that picture of the potential animal nature of man, is now reinforced by the dragon.

Perhaps we can put it like this: the dragon in his double nature, as Devil and Satan, as Lucifer and Ahriman, presents his power and his own temptation in two different stages. As Lucifer, the 'old serpent', we read in Genesis his temptation was formulated thus: 'You will be like God, knowing good and evil.' That was the first stage. Now the other half, shall we say, the Ahriman half, is well aware that we have known a good deal about good and evil, and the temptation is now: 'You may be like the beast, like the animal, and need no longer bother about good and evil.' This perhaps is a way in which the dragon, with his *second* nature, gives of his power and his seat and his authority to this beast in which we saw the animal nature of man rising out of the sea of his blood and bodily juices.

But to complete our study, we must finally say a word about the second beast, described later in the chapter, in the eleventh verse.

> And I beheld another beast coming up out of the earth; and he had two horns like a lamb, and he spake as a dragon.

And then, right at the end of the chapter,

> Here is wisdom. Let him that hath understanding count the number of the beast: for it is the number of a man; and his number is Six hundred and three score and six.

That is another beast, and certainly without Steiner's help in the matter I would not really know very well what to make of it. I know that theological scholars have tried to dissolve the number 666 into letters, whereby one could say it reads: *Nero.* This puts us right back in the Roman Empire, and we dealt with that problem in a general way earlier on, as you may remember. But this is not the whole story, and here now I draw on Steiner's esoteric research. He verifies that there is indeed a beast of this kind, a spiritual entity, and he also deciphers the number 666 into letters. His interpretation confirms certain traditions in the Jewish Cabbala, so that one reads the name as Sorath, and this is, in the tradition of the ancient world, a demonic being that dwells in the sun sphere.* This is a being not so closely connected with man as the first beast, although man can give way to him, but a being with quite definite anti-Christian intentions and powers. Steiner explains that this being, Sorath, was known in esoteric circles by a particular sign, and he suggests that the description of the two-horned beast really refers to this 'horned' occult symbol.

Already in the second lecture we mentioned the significance of 666 in relation to the evolution of the earth in the distant future.† It may also be of interest to look back into post-Christian historical times to particular *dates* in connection with this number.

Round about A.D. 666, the first great, really successful anti-Christian movement entered our civilisation in the form of Mohammedanism. This says, of course, nothing against some of the great moral teachings of Mohammedanism, the wonderful culture, architecture and science connected with it, but it was as if Mohammed and his followers, as a friend of mine used to say, made God into a sultan, who has no son, and human life subject to *kismet*, to fatalism, creating a

* For Rudolf Steiner's explanation of this, see Lecture XI in his lectures *The Apocalypse of St. John*.

† See p. 47 and also Rudolf Steiner, *The Apocalypse of St. John*, particularly Lecture XI.

religion in which individual creative freedom has no place.

Twice 666 came in 1332. At about that time the beast manifested itself in the persecution of the Knights Templars. Under torture they spoke ghastly blasphemies against Christ, which, of course, they immediately recanted afterwards. Rudolf Steiner says that the tortures were so arranged that Sorath spoke his blasphemies through the mouths of the tortured Templars. They were the victims of an alliance between Philip le Bel of France and a weak pope. What was the reason? Ostensibly, heresy. But they had become the bankers of the world. They were such trustworthy people that the princes, the cities and the monastic orders deposited their gold with them. The Templars *knew* the *danger* of gold and they had the spiritual wisdom so to administer it that it would not have turned to the detriment of the human race as it is doing today. But they were persecuted, the gold was taken from them, and we read the fantastic story of how Philip le Bel of France *bathed* in gold; he had gold amassed and sat in it, and drew his beastly inspirations from living, bathing in gold.

Three times 666 is not quite Orwell's 1984, but 1998. Rudolf Steiner spoke in the last few months of his life, beginning only in July 1924 in a series of lectures in Arnhem in Holland,* of the significance of that year. He said that a vital confrontation will take place again when the destiny of the human race will be decided for centuries to come.

I believe that when we read the Apocalypse, albeit

* Rudolf Steiner, *Karmic Relationships*, Vol. VI, Rudolf Steiner Press, London, 1971.

in this naturally very tentative and imperfect way, we nevertheless move in a sphere where these things can be to some extent integrated, and where at least a number of human souls are willing to look at these things with an understanding which is indeed folly in the mental climate of our age, but which, on the other hand, can link us with the *depths* of this century. And we shall take our place in it if we once again remember that the great truth towards which we move is, in terms of this twelfth chapter, that the soul is coming back from her loneliness, her wilderness, and that the child descends; the *real* ego of man begins to enter in. It may take a whole life, it may take more than one incarnation for it to achieve its purpose, but it is about to happen. In that process we must learn to turn the two-edged sword of the ego, about which we spoke some weeks ago, into the wand made of starry steel: strong, unbreakable, flexible and resilient, but also in harmony with the stars from which its stuff has been taken.

Babylon the Prostitute – Jerusalem the Bride

Anyone who has had the patience to follow these talks may now have a series of questions and comments. It would be unnatural if that were not so. There is certainly one serious criticism possible about my approach to our subject. Since the book moves constantly towards moments of crisis, we are constantly called upon to make moral decisions, we are challenged to take a line, to declare our loyalty; and I am sure it could be said that this paramount element in the book has been, if not entirely neglected, at least underplayed in my talks hitherto. The reason for this, rightly or wrongly, is quite simple. I believe that in most of the commentaries one can read this particular aspect is rather *over*stressed, and, of course, there is a certain temptation to do so, because it is the underlying motive power of the book that emerges time and again. By stressing that, however, and trying to get that particular message across, one can then lump together other details and perhaps pass over them too quickly.

My own endeavour has been somewhat different: to select representative sections – (it has hardly been possible to do more than select, as one cannot discuss every verse in seven evenings) – and this has allowed us to deal with a number of details and make an attempt to decode the book's mysterious language, which, as we pointed out on a previous occasion, is in itself no more mysterious than a book of chemistry with its formulae or a book with the equations of the mathematical physicist are to the uninitiated. But *now*, finally, this paramount theme must come to the fore, must emerge. We are faced with that final vision which puts before our spiritual eye the great alternatives: Babylon, the doomed city and the great cosmic catastrophe on the one hand, and the New Jerusalem, the wonderful picture of a cosmic transformation, on the other. And we are, of course, by implication, challenged to choose between Babylon and Jerusalem.

Here again lies one of the interesting differences from the vision of world evolution as it has been presented in recent times by Teilhard de Chardin, whose work calls for great interest and study. On a previous occasion, we said that while he describes with beautiful and moving language the movement of our world towards what he calls the Omega point, he is less clear about the Alpha point. And today we can note that as his Omega point is more or less leading into one great cosmic transformation, perhaps his archaeological training overlays the clarity of his spiritual vision. We must remember the two-edged sword that we considered earlier, which, in Steiner's explanation, is a picture for the double-edged nature of the human ego, which produces at the end the double-edged finality of that section of cosmic development with which the Book of Revelation presents us. We have a two-edged culmination: a wonderful transformation and a cosmic catastrophe.

The idea of a cosmic catastrophe occurring in the

course of human evolution, in the evolution of our world, is neither peculiar to the Book of Revelation nor in itself new. The idea that the accumulated wickedness of the human race reaches such a tension, such a boiling point, that it interferes with the balance of nature is, for instance, inherent in all the stories connected with the great Flood, with the doom of Atlantis. Occult tradition in general, confirmed by the independent research of Rudolf Steiner, does speak of what one might call the 'fall-out' of the accumulated wickedness of the human race at a certain time in the Atlantean period, which upset the balance of nature and produced the flood that destroyed the Atlantic continent. It is described in homely terms in the Bible, and just in order to have a sufficiently wide backcloth for our description of the fall of Babylon, I will read a few verses from the sixth chapter of *Genesis:*

> And God saw that the wickedness of man was great in the earth and that every imagination of the thoughts of his heart was only evil continually. And it repented the Lord that he had made man on the earth, and it grieved him at his heart. . . . And God said unto Noah, The end of all flesh is come before me: for the earth is filled with violence through them; and, behold, I will destroy them with the earth.

If we compare the Book of Revelation, the last book in the Bible, with the first one from which I have just read, we see that the envisaged catastrophe is not of flood, but of fire, in which what is called Babylon is engulfed.

What then is Babylon? In the title I chose the rather startling phrase, 'Babylon the Prostitute', for Babylon is described in the Book of Revelation as the mother of harlots, as the scarlet woman and with a variety of other terms of the same kind. Now it is clear to all scholars that these terms are not used literally; they are a type of language which describe much more a kind of general idolatry, a kind of 'whoring after strange gods' to use another Biblical phrase. It was really the nineteenth century that was interested in the scarlet woman aspect as such, and emphasised it, and tried to make God into a kind of puritan moralist. The terms used speak of a more comprehensive, more far-reaching type of evil and wickedness; and we are led to the discovery of that sphere by the very fact that both Babylon *and* Jerusalem are described as women. This turns our thoughts back to the other great mythological conception, that at the very beginning of things was a woman, the great Mother, the Mother Earth, the Ur-Mater, Materia – (all these words are interconnected and carry with them a whole complex of connotations and associations). The fundamental core of the Babylonian wickedness is its attitude to matter. You see, matter, material existence as we know it, is the great gift of this present planetary stage of evolution. If I may, I will recall to your minds matters we have mentioned on previous occasions: that in occult tradition one speaks of the various planetary transformations of our universe as the Saturn stage, the Sun stage, the Moon stage and the Earth stage. You will remember last time we spoke of the Moon stage of the earth as being liquid, not rigid, not yet firm, whereas in our present stage of evolution we deal with firm ground, with matter, with hard, rigid matter. Our relationship to matter, therefore, as human beings in the present cosmic day is of the greatest significance; it is crucial.

134

It is, of course, easy to say we should not be given to belief in material values, put them before spiritual values, sell our higher self for thirty pieces of silver, get involved in material ambitions and strive for absolute material power. These are all aspects of the problem, but by Babylonian standards they are still in the forecourt of the whole problem. It is, I am almost tempted to say, our *religious* attitude to matter that is called in question, and, in order to lead our thoughts into this perhaps somewhat unexpected and not altogether easy territory, I refer again to that great scientist, Francis Bacon, who said that the human soul can be extended to comprehend the mysteries, but that the mysteries cannot be constricted to suit the narrowness of the human soul. But he wielded the double-edged sword if anyone did, and among the problematic directives for the rising scientific development, he said: 'We must put nature on the rack, and extort from nature the answers in which we are interested'. He is the father of this inquisitorial attitude which experimental science has practised in its research into nature, the attitude that upset Goethe so much. He advocated quite a different attitude; he said that our relationship to nature should be like the relationship of a lover to his beloved, who is willing to listen to the confidences she is willing to give him. You can see the radical difference of approach, and to some extent the radical difference of the *result* of this approach to nature.

Generally speaking, our Western mind has followed the Baconian attitude, and there we can observe the first faint beginnings of the Babylonian attitude: the inquisitorial treatment of nature, the exploitation of nature for man's exclusive benefit. This approach, of course, has produced a very lop-sided popular world-picture. Those of you who want to follow this up in greater detail I would like to direct to a book by Dr. Ernst Lehrs, published in this country under the title, *Man or Matter*,* which gives a really comprehensive picture of the essential one-sidedness, the one-eyed, colour-blind view, of our present mind in our observation of nature.

In order to drive the point home, I will select one or two outstanding events of more recent times. I think it will be useful as it will bring the whole question of the Babylonian idolatry much closer home to us than would otherwise be the case. One example, I think, is the release of atomic energy – quite apart from the use we make of it. Let us imagine Goethe were alive and what he would say, what would be his attitude as an *artist*-scientist towards this. I believe he would first of all explain the whole set of chemical elements, the periodic table. As far as lead, in their atomic weight, the elements behave in a natural and stable manner, but then you come down to heavier atomic weight, to the heavy metals, ultimately to uranium; and there metal begins to behave in a rather queer way. Matter is no longer quite stable – (the physicists speak of metastability). It is there that fission is possible. Man has observed this and has learned a method of speeding it up, of combing out the heavier isotope and producing plutonium. The tricks he has learned with this he is now able to apply to practically all the elements right up to hydrogen. This is all extraordinarily interesting, but it is outside what I imagine

* Faber & Faber, London, 1951.

Goethe would call the ordinary decent behaviour of the normal elements. He would not, I think, suggest that it should not be done, but he would want human beings to make a moral evaluation of it, and that moral evaluation would not only be concerned with the use of atomic energy itself, either constructive or destructive, but with the whole process. There, we have gone *very* far with our inquisitorial approach. We are on the point, as I once heard someone say, of tearing the guts out of matter.

This, however, is only one field. I by-pass another, where we treat nature and matter rather arbitrarily – the whole artificiality of food production and the adulteration of food-stuffs, the whole sphere of artificial fabrics, plastic material, where nature is tortured with almost unimaginable degrees of heat and pressure. Let us instead go to the latest of these problems which was dealt with in last Sunday's colour supplement to *The Observer*, in relation to the book that has just appeared with the title *The Biological Time-Bomb.**
It deals with the fact that we are on the verge of being able now not only to get to the very centre and heart, to the guts of inorganic matter, but to the heart of *life*. We are not very far from the moment when we can really produce a mutation in the genes, and can thereby influence the normal heredity; we can gradually visualise a moment when we can so influence by electronic means, by radiations, by other subtle biochemical methods, that we can in this semi-mechanical way produce, as they say, the *ideal man*. The question is raised: Who decides what the ideal man should be?

* Gordon Rattray Taylor: *The Biological Time-Bomb*. Thames and Hudson, London, 1968.

The bio-chemist himself? Or perhaps the government on the majority vote in the House of Commons? You see where it leads to. But you can also see that those things exercise a tremendous fascination, not only on the research worker, but on those who read and listen. These are the matters that today are absorbed through the mass-media; these are the matters that produce, to use the Biblical phrase, Gog and Magog, which is simply the Hebrew way of expressing 'collective' – the small collective and the big collective. It is the fascination of these things where the greatest danger lies, because one can be passionately involved in them. On one or two occasions when Rudolf Steiner spoke, with very grave words, on these developments – (they did not happen in his day, but he had a notion that they might happen) – he used a rather startling phrase concerning the mentality that results from involvement in these matters; he called it *Gedanken-Sodomiterei*, a kind of sodomy of thought. There is in the absorption in these matters a kind of perverted sexual flavour, and this is perhaps as far as I would go in this talk to show where the *link* lies with the traditional conception of Babylon.

Babylon, in the Apocalyptic view, is a picture of a civilisation in which these matters are cultivated, enhanced and furthered, and it would certainly be wrong and perhaps even foolish to suggest that what has happened hitherto has already the hall-mark of the Beast. But, after all, Rudolf Steiner says the 'division' begins in this century, and I believe such things as I have pointed out certainly call for a moral evaluation. It can never be a question of simply 'dropping' them; one cannot turn the clock back. (And if Chesterton

138

answered that the obvious answer to that is that you *can*, well, of course, then your clock is out, it shows the wrong time). No, you cannot do that but, and this is what Rudolf Steiner pleaded for, there must be *counter-measures* to *balance* this development; and he came back time and again to this conception: the only remedy, the only source of balance for this is the rediscovery of the reality of Christ – His energy, His presence, His reality in the world as something which exists. This is a difficult matter if one views the world as it is; perhaps the nearest approach in the right direction is among people like the present Bishop of Woolwich* and his school, saying that what they want is a Christianity without religion; which is a very good thing – to seek the real Christ, as a cosmic being, as a source of living energy, entirely independent of all the dead weight of traditional Christianity.

Here Steiner's approach to this grave matter and the implication of the Book of Revelation come together, because that is also what the book really asks us to strive for: to meet the Christ as a spiritual reality in our cosmos, in the world in which we move. This really *is* the counter-balance, because from that source, in terms of power, in terms of guidance, and in terms of inspiration, the direction comes that allows us to live in a world in which these things happen and that allows us to resist being drawn into the vortex of the beginning of the civilisation of Babylon. It is the real central attitude to matter, be it organic or inorganic, that is at stake. It is not, although it is involved to some extent, a question of the usual sins and

* John A. T. Robinson. (His book, *Honest to God*, SCM Press, London, 1963).

139

trespasses and wickednesses of human beings. In that respect, possibly, there is some progress, but, although it may seem strange to the ordinary moralist, and grievous as these matters may be, the mark of Babylon is in that *other* field.

However, there is a comfort in the beginning of one of Steiner's lectures* on the Apocalypse, in which he says this possibility of meeting the Christ and drawing on His presence will return time and again, and that it needs a very determined attitude to refuse it. This is what he says:

> . . . in the future the Earth with all its beings will pass into a kind of spiritual condition, with the exception of those who refuse to receive the Christ-principle;

He is always careful to call it the *Christ-principle* to avoid confusion with Christianity as a religion.

> this refusal we have to understand as a malevolent and unintelligent spiritual opposition energetically exercised.

It is, as he said once, a difficult job to be deliberately evil; but the possibility does exist.

I should also like to read to you a few lines which have just been published in honour of the seventieth birthday of Berthold Brecht which, in my translation, read like this: 'On my wall hangs a Japanese sculpture in wood, mask of a bad demon, laquered in gold. With concern, I observe the swollen arteries in the forehead; they indicate how strenuous it is to be evil'.

Now it is strange, when we have just looked into the darkness of the abyss, to find that the final catastrophe that engulfs Babylon is lamented in the Book of Revelation by what I believe to be the most moving

* Lecture XI.

lament in the whole of the world's literature. You can see how grand the book is: it has to foretell what will happen, and yet it laments it. As it is the last evening, I take the liberty of reading that lament to you in my own translation. Let me first just formulate the catastrophe once more in a simple sentence. Rudolf Steiner made a statement of twelve sentences of basic Christian truth which are read as a kind of creed in the Communion service of The Christian Community. The sentence I should like to quote runs thus: 'Then He (the Christ) will in time unite for the advancement of the world with those who through their bearing He can wrest from the death of matter'. That is, perhaps, the neatest formulation of the death of Matter and the way in which human beings can be wrested from it.

And now here is the incredible lament in Chapter 18.

> After this I saw another angel coming down from heaven endowed with great power and authority, and the very earth shone with the splendour of his being. His voice rang out and he cried: 'Fallen, fallen is Babylon the Great! She has become a haunt of demons and a prison of every foul spirit, and a cage of every ominous and hateful bird. For all the nations have drunk of the wine of her passionate apostacy, and the kings of the earth have practised idolatry with her, and the merchants of the earth have grown rich from the recklessness of her dissipation.'
>
> And I heard another voice from heaven say, 'Come out of her, O my people, lest you be drawn into the community of her sins and must share the blows of her fate. For her sins have mounted up to the heavens, and God has called to mind the record of her wickedness. Give her back what she has given you; give her back double for what she has done. In the cup that she mixed for others, mix her a drink of twice the strength. For her self-glorification and self-indulgence,

give her purging torture and grief in equal measure. For she says in her heart: "Here I am seated a queen; I am no lonely widow, and I shall never know sorrow." Therefore in a single day her fate shall strike her – death, grief and famine, and she shall be burned in the fire. For stern and strong is the Lord who passes judgement on her.'

And the kings of the earth who indulged with her in idolatry and wild extravagance will wail and beat their breasts over her when they see the smoke of her burning. Standing far off, terrified by her fateful trial, they cry, 'Alas, alas, for that great city, for Babylon the mighty city, that in one single hour the crisis should come upon you!'

And the merchants of the earth shall also wail and grieve over her, for there is no one left to buy their goods – cargoes of gold and silver and jewels and pearls and fine linen and purple and silk and scarlet, and all kinds of scented wood, and every kind of ivory vessel, every kind of vessel of most precious wood, of brass, iron and marble; cinnamon, spice, fine flour and corn; cattle and sheep, horses and chariots, and the bodies and souls of men.

'The fruit of the harvest which your heart desired is gone from you for ever; all your finery and brilliance are lost to you and none of it will be found any more.'

The merchants of these goods who have grown wealthy from her will stand far off, terrified by her fateful trial, weeping and lamenting and saying: 'Alas, alas, for the great city, that was dressed in fine linen, and purple and scarlet, and covered with gold, jewels and pearls! For in one single hour all this great wealth has turned into waste land.'

And every shipmaster and crew, all sailors and others whose business is upon the sea, stood far off and cried out when they saw the smoke of her burning: 'What city was ever like the great city?' And they threw dust upon their heads, weeping and lamenting, and cried: 'Alas, alas, for the great city where all who have ships upon the sea grew rich from her treasure. For in one single hour she is laid waste.' . . .

And that one mighty angel lifted up a stone like a great

millstone and threw it into the sea saying, 'Thus with a mighty sweep shall Babylon, the great city, be flung down, and shall never more be found. Never again shall the sound of harpists or musicians, or flute players or trumpeters be heard in you. Never again shall a craftsman of any craft be found in you, nor the sound of the grinding of the millstone be heard in you. No light of lamp shall ever shine in you again, nor the voice of the bridegroom nor the bride be heard in you any more.

'Indeed, your merchants were the great ones of the earth, and all the nations of the earth were thrown off their course by the spell of your magic.'

The blood of prophets and saints was discovered in her, and the blood of all others ever shed on the earth in sacrifice.

Looking at Babylon, we have seen the vast measurements, the cosmic dimensions, in which all this has to be understood, and we can now put this to good use when we turn in the other direction to the New Jerusalem. There is, to start with, a striking difference in the description: Babylon is described almost *entirely* in terms of a woman; very little is said about the city itself. The view is concentrated on what might have been, perhaps, the wicked soul of that time. We are told that the beast tears strips off her clothes, that every pretence of finery is taken away from her, and her real self, such as it is, emerges. With the New Jerusalem there is practically no description of a woman; she is simply called 'the bride adorned for her husband'. But the *city*, the place where you can *dwell*, is described in beautiful and moving detail: the streets all gold, but gold clear as glass, translucent gold; the walls founded on twelve precious stones, in which are inscribed the names of the twelve apostles; the twelve gates with twelve angels watching over them and the names of the twelve tribes of Israel inscribed on them. We see how twelve, which we have come to understand as the number of space, now dominates the scene. The light in the city is described as the light that blazed from the throne in the vision of the abiding Presence in the fourth chapter. In that city there is the River of Life, and the Tree of Life restored; there is no church, no temple, because the presence of God is paramount. One can understand how this wonderful vision has been such a great comfort to poor and distressed souls through the years the Bible has been available to the people. You will know how many hymns were written with the element of the New Jerusalem in them, the pearly gates and golden streets, and all the rather dazzling, and at the same time comforting, picture of the Holy City.

And now, what leads to the Holy City? Just as little as, on the one hand, ordinary sins and trespasses, but something deeper, lead to Babylon, so not just ordinary goodness and decency, although they are most definitely included, make the whole of the New Jerusalem. It is again the basic attitude of the human being to the sacred gift of earth evolution, to matter. Here Goethe really emerges as a prophet of the New Jerusalem. His approach to nature, as a scientist-artist, as an artist-scientist, as a lover, listening to what she has to say, really sets the example for the attitude that builds the New Jerusalem. It is the attitude of the great artist, the one who discovers the *pieta* slumbering in the marble, who does not impress his own conception on the piece of stone, but finds what is dormant in it, the great artist who finds what is dormant in the colours with which he works. But this attitude can also extend right down to little things, wherever there is love for material – to furniture and carpets and curtains, and the visualisation of the tea-pot that sleeps in the clay – wherever something is made as an act of redemption, as an act of *elevating* matter rather than using it simply for human exploitation and profit. It is a fundamental artistic attitude; I know we cannot keep it up, it is impossible, but there are little things in daily life in relation to which we can practise it so that it does not *die* in us. 'Let the artist not die in your soul' is perhaps a message coming from the New Jerusalem.

That can also apply to human relationships, where there is a great space for real art. In the opening verses of the chapters on the New Jerusalem, the One from the throne explains: 'Behold, I make all things new.' This is one of the most beautiful and fruitful moral mottoes one can think about. 'I make all things new.' In other words, you can always start again. As long as there is life on earth, this should be known, and that is, in a way, the attitude of the citizen of the New Jerusalem in his human relationships; they may go wrong, but, 'Behold, I make all things new.' A new start is always possible; it may be different, but it is always possible. Finally, however, on the highest level, it is the attitude we take towards that most precious bit of matter, our own body. If the New Jerusalem teaches us one thing, it teaches us *not* to despise our body, *not* to mortify it, or think of it as a horrible thing we have to carry round with us. No, this is the material where work can and should begin.

In the actual imagery used to describe the city, there are certain indications for those who can read them; the Cabbala has tradition about it, and Rudolf

145

Steiner also, independently, spoke about it. For instance, the twelve precious stones which are the foundation stones of the city walls are the transformed senses of the human being, the five more obvious senses and the seven more occult ones. We work towards this transformation to start with by training our ordinary senses to observe, as selflessly as we can, nature and the world around us, to take an interest in them. The word 'interest', from the Latin *inter esse*, means 'to be in or between'. You enter into things with your loving concern. The pearls are also a symbol. You know how a pearl comes into being in nature; a foreign body enters into a shell-fish and hurts it, but instead of being thrown off it is transformed into a thing of beauty. That is how pain, how frustrations are to be treated – to be turned into pearls. We may not succeed, but there is the direction.

Or we take another striking but rather puzzling description. The measurements of the city are given in different ways, and they do not square. On the one hand, they are given in outline: 'And the city lieth four-square, and the length is as large as the breadth; and he measured the city with the reed, twelve thousand furlongs.' Then comes this very difficult passage: 'The length and the breadth and the *height* of it are equal. And he measured the wall thereof, an hundred and forty and four cubits, according to the measure of a man, that is, of the angel.' Now, there is mystical language. In this particular sentence the city is imagined as a tremendous cube, and this is said to be 'the measure of a man', but it is also the measure of an angel. We may say it becomes the measure of a man the moment the man has attained a particular quality of the angel, which is to *breathe* differently. As we breathe normally, we breathe *in* the breath of life and breathe *out* the breath of death. We know, as I have often pointed out, that if we sealed all the doors and windows hermetically, and just sat quietly here, by tomorrow morning we should all be dead – simply by breathing out carbon-dioxide. One of the great transformations that the human body can finally go through is that of the transformation of the breath, so that ultimately we would breathe out the breath of life – pure carbon. Carbon left to itself forms a cube; it is the raw material of all organic things, of all life.

So you see, even if I select only this one instance, that the picture of the golden city is full of mystery on many levels. It is beautiful as it is; it takes up where the Garden of Eden left off, with the Tree of Life and the River of Life, but it has these almost alchemistic mysteries in it to show what can be done and how the human body has something to do with it.

And now, for the last few minutes, what I should like to be able to convey to you really involves the presenting of a mystery; it is one of the most moving and profound things that you find in Steiner's teaching, to which he returns time and again. He tells how, already today, through *man* the foundations of the new world are laid, already today, what he calls the Jupiter state, the next stage of planetary evolution, is actually set in motion; the New Jerusalem is potentially there in certain human attitudes; they need not be grand, but they are concerned with the love of matter, the love of renewal, the love of the redemption and transformation of the bodily instrument. Again, one comes back to the simple fact: the pattern for all this is the

Christ. He, apart from and above everything else, dealt in this matter with the body of Jesus. He was the first who, through the transformation of the body of Jesus, laid the foundation stone, or, if you like, the blueprint of the New Jerusalem. The tremendous fact that He so *loved* his body that He could transform it, that after Golgotha He turned it into a resurrection body, into a source of energy and strength so that there was no corpse left behind – that is the supreme achievement, and that is what ultimately man can move towards; he, the first Adam.

It has been pointed out that the Bible begins with the description of a garden, the Garden of Eden, and ends with the description of a city, the New Jerusalem; man is involved in it. The way from the Garden to the City would not, however, be possible if between there were not also a garden with an empty tomb. The man who saw these three pictures together saw a great wisdom, a great mystery. Today, we are really at the cross-roads where opting for Babylon or the New Jerusalem is no longer a matter for consideration by some small religious groups, but is a vital matter for all the most advanced, the most responsible, the most educated men and women, because it is really the *leadership* of our world that is at stake.

Rudolf Steiner said that the Book of Revelation is a book of training for the will, it is a book for the initiation through the will. Now initiations through the will are difficult, almost impossible for us today. One can understand that perhaps men of earlier ages without the natural mental inhibitions that we have could read the book, perhaps even 'eat' it, and were then so stimulated, so grasped by it, so absorbed in it in their will-forces that at the end, quite simply, the New Jerusalem was before them and they declared their loyalty in that direction. We cannot do that; we need to go into it, step by step, in an attempt to understand, and it is that of course to which I hoped I would be able to make some contribution in these talks. There is a great deal in the book that we have *not* touched, and there is a great deal that, even if we *had* touched it, I would not have been able to present in a way that made sense. At least we have opened the doors and removed some of the barriers resulting from our normal twentieth-century mentality, so that ultimately our wills really can be challenged, and we really can opt, exercise our discretion, one way or the other. And with this in mind, we may well perhaps, very humbly, conclude these talks with two verses from the last chapter.

> And he said unto me, These sayings are faithful and true: and the Lord God of the holy prophets sent his angel to show to his servants the things which must shortly be done.
> Behold, I come quickly: blessed is he that keepeth the sayings of the prophecy of this book.

Questions and answers were recorded after this lecture. See p. 155.

ANSWERS TO QUESTIONS
ASKED AFTER THE LECTURES

First lecture, p. 13

I.

Asked if one could view the opening of the Book of Revelation
as a condensed account of things that would happen, Dr.
Heidenreich said that it did not seem to be precisely a prophecy
of particular, individual events; rather the book described *typical*
events which could happen *at any time*. He referred again to
Steiner who, speaking of history in general, said that we *dream*
history. '*Die Geschichte ist ein Weltentraum der Menschheit.*'
'History is a cosmic dream of humanity.' Dr. Heidenreich went
on to say: Interestingly enough, only a few weeks ago I came
across an almost similar statement by Lytton Strachey who said,
'Dreams are the essence of history'. This is quoted in the
introduction by Rolf Hochhut to his play *The Representative*
(about Churchill and Sikorsky). Really a good deal of the great
events of history are just *dreamed* by us, and the Book of
Revelation is to some extent a kind of permanent cosmic dream,
but a *very* active dream, which goes on, and into which at times
we can enter, and which in part then we can read, and from
which we can be inspired. It is the sort of thing which possibly,
unconsciously, we share in a good deal during the night, because
one of the great problems for modern man is that we forget that
something happens in sleep, apart from our being just unconscious. In sleep we enter deeply into that sphere where these
dreams, these great world dreams are taking place, or are
dreamt. I think it is in that sense that perhaps one could say the
book as it is written is a sort of concentrate taken out of this.
But it is very much of a unit.

II.

Question: How old would the St. John who wrote the Book of
Revelation have been in the year 95?

Answer: If one thinks of him as a contemporary of Christ, or just a little younger, he would have been in his early nineties.

Question: Would someone of his age have been capable of writing with his own hand such a long work?

Answer: This raises a very complicated question. In the first chapter John says that he is an exile in Patmos, and it is generally assumed that he was exiled there during the Domitian persecution in 95. But the way in which these revelations were committed to writing is a great mystery. The same question arises about the Gospels – whether the evangelists wrote with their own hands, whether they dictated, or whether they conceived them in their memory and recited them from time to time and then other people gradually remembered them and took them down. Generally speaking, we are becoming more and more willing to understand that the retentive memory of earlier centuries was far greater than our own. The very fact that we can read and write to some extent undermines our memory. If on one day you tell children a fairy story, even children of three or four, and then tell the same story slightly differently a few days later, they correct you, because immediately the sequence of words sticks in their minds, particularly if there is a certain amount of rhythm to them. And even today, the retentive memory of primitive tribes is very great indeed. One assumes, for instance, that even Homer's *Iliad* and *Odessey* were recited for almost centuries by wandering bards, until the time came when it was felt the memory no longer sufficed and they had to be written down. Some such development is likely to be what happened to the Book of Revelation. Although the ancient masters always painted John sitting on a little island writing away with the eagle above him, that is pious imagination. It was probably there that the Apocalypse came into being, and on special occasions he may have recited it.

III.

Question: Dr. Heidenreich, did you say the Apocalypse was written *after* the Epistles and the Gospels?

Answer: There again, it is very difficult to say. Sometimes it is thought that even the Gospel is the last of the three. The Epistles one can date a little more accurately, and they may be a little earlier. But whether the Apocalypse or the Gospel is the very last one, it would be very difficult to say. But they were both probably 'written' at the far end of John's mature life.

Third lecture, p. 54

I.

Question: Did John actually say that he saw a ram or a lamb on the throne?*

Answer: The Greek is *arnion* (actually neuter), but it does really mean 'ram'.

Question: Does it have the same connotation of sacrifice, humility and meekness?

Answer: Oh, indeed yes. Even a ram can make a sacrifice.

Question: That is interesting, but 'ram' suggests a rather fierce animal, doesn't it? Whereas it is much more possible to associate 'lamb' with the idea of humility and gentleness.

Answer: There is something in that, although on the other hand I think we have got too much used to thinking of the Lamb of God as just very meek. The Lamb of God is a *tremendously* powerful being,† you know, yet in all that power, 'obedient unto death' as Paul says. There is tension. The achievement tends to be minimised if one thinks of the Lamb as the rather meek being we normally do. That is why I am rather keen on stressing the other element of it.

Another member of the audience: There is a sonnet of John Donne in which Ram and Lamb are used in two consecutive lines:

> O strong Ramme, which hast batter'd heaven for mee,
> Mild Lambe, which with thy blood, hast mark'd the
> path . . .‡

Answer: Thank you very much! That is wonderful.

* See footnote on p. 57.   † See for example Rev. 17:14.
‡ From Donne's Holy Sonnets, La Corona, No. 7, *Ascension.*

II.

Question: I always think of the number twelve in connection with space, and you mentioned that the twenty-four elders have to do with time.

Answer: The cycles of time do come to twice twelve, but we shall see twelve next time as the number of space. Generally speaking, as a good guiding thought, seven can be taken as the number of time and twelve as the number of space, but there is never absolutely quite such a dividing line. You see, the connecting link is that, although these twenty-four can be seen as what Steiner calls the '*Regler*', the regulators of the cosmic clock, at the same time, of course, these twenty-four periods are ordered according to the order of *space* as the sun goes twice round the zodiac. This is really where the great picture of space presented by the twelvehood of the zodiac overlaps with the sequence of time, because the time is ordered according to the order of space in this case.

III.

Question: Must the Lamb of God always be sacrificed, and must there always be human sacrifice, too?

Answer: I think that begs a little the question what a 'sacrifice' is. It started obviously in the cosmic significance of Christ's Incarnation, and Golgotha as a full sacrifice in the sense of the phrase, 'sacrifice unto death'. But gradually the significance of sacrifice becomes wider and perhaps, shall I say, less cruel? But I think we all know from experience that it is almost the only means of real growth – until ultimately we do not call it sacrifice any more, but the sacrifice turns into pleasure, not in a perverted sense, but in the sense in which this particular acclamation says.

Question: Also, when you say 'God' – what is the conception we have to accept of God?

Answer: I have no 'conception' of God at all. I think it is one of the very last things. . . . At the moment, really, what we can gain once more is a gradual realisation of a spiritual world. That spiritual world is inhabited by a 'company of heaven' so to speak, of spiritual beings who have their particular functions and status etcetera, and the conception of monotheism does not merely mean the belief in one god, but the realisation of the unity of the spiritual world. And that is perhaps about as close at the moment as one can come to the conception of a god – in the same way as you can do it in yourself. You see, you have the sense of an 'I' which gives you the idea of a unity of your own being. The more, in a way, you open yourself and study and experience, the more, of course, you know how incredibly complicated you are – on *every* level. You can take physiology – the human body is fantastic in its functions. At a pinch you can learn the names of the bones, and perhaps the muscles, but the moment the body goes into action, it becomes fantastically complicated. Then consider all that goes with life; as soon as you study the phenomena of life in us, not only their reflection in a physiological way, but life as it were itself, our contact with other human beings, you come into the whole intense region of the emotions etcetera, and then you touch on the inner sphere of the spirit – well, you may be very grateful if you can realise that in this microcosm there is a unity, and if you grasp the sense of that unity, you have a kind of reflection of what we call 'God', what God may mean to the spiritual world.

Seventh lecture, p. 131
I.
Question: Is awareness of the Etheric Christ a matter of individual growth?
Answer: The way in which that real Presence either manifests itself or how we approach that sphere is individually very different. It can be given by grace; it can be the result of very earnest work and development. When St. Paul in his letter to the Thessalonians speaks of Christ coming in the clouds – (which we read to be the Etheric Christ) – he says we will be lifted up into the air to meet Christ there. It is, of course, a way of describing that there is a two-way process; we move towards that experience with our endeavour, and the

experience meets us on the way, but where exactly that point is presumably is different with different people.

II.

Question: You mentioned that in this age the way to initiation is not really through the will.

Answer: Not through the will *unless* you have the consciousness fully clear within it.

Question: Would you say it was more through the realm of feeling?

Answer: No. It is through thought. The modern way of initiation is the transformation of thought. The medieval way was through feeling, and a quite specific technique of an initiation through the will-forces is found in the Jesuit exercises. They are quite specifically designed to engage the will in a special direction; but the modern initiation which leaves you completely free and does not make you dependent on anything or anybody is the transformation of thought.

Question: The artistic side of man, though, is really more concerned with feeling, isn't it? We are warned in this not to lose sight of the artistic side.

Answer: Yes, but even that, you see, needs to be co-ordinated today. When I say 'thinking' I do not refer to the analytical intellect which pulls everything to pieces, but to a comprehension of the great basic realities of existence, which, by their very nature, will inspire you to artistic deeds, and in doing them you engage the whole gamut of your feelings. And in order, then, finally to bring your inspiration to expression you engage your will, but it is directed from a clear consciousness.

III.

Question: I was wondering how Babylon came to be given as the name for these evil forces. Was that civilisation particularly prone to put nature on the rack?

Answer: I think there are two answers to that. One that is generally given by Biblical scholars is that it is simply taken from the old story of the Tower of Babel, where there was a kind of manifestation of revolt against the divine order. Rudolf Steiner gives an additional explanation, saying that Babylon at a certain time of its history was given over to very questionable occult practices – a kind of mediumistic type of practices bordering on Black Magic. That was probably in the air when the book was written. Ultimately, you can say the difference between Babylon and Jerusalem is the difference between Black Magic and White Magic. Ultimately, the dealing with matter becomes a magic practice; it can be constructive magic practice, a transformation into goodness; it can be the opposite.

THE BOOK OF REVELATION

An English rendering by Alfred Heidenreich

Chapter 1

This is the revelation of Christ Jesus which God, the Father Ground of the World, has given him in order to show those who serve him what is to come and what is approaching at a quickening pace.

He has set it out in pictures and sent it through his angel to his servant John who was an eye-witness of the Word who had come from God and of the martyrdom of Jesus Christ.

Blessed is he who reads the words of this prophecy, those who listen and ponder the things which are written in it. For the time is at hand.

*   *   *

John to the seven churches in Asia:

> grace and peace be to you from him
> who is
> who was
> and who will be,

and from the seven Creator-Spirits before his throne, and from Jesus Christ,

> the faithful witness,
> the first-born from the realm of the dead,
> the principal of all the rulers of the earth.

To him who loves us, who through the power of his blood frees us from the sickness of sin, and who has made us to be a kingdom, and priests for God his father, to him be glory and power through all cycles of time. Amen.

See, he comes in the realm of the clouds. Every eye shall see him, even those who pierced him. Men of every kind on the earth shall be shaken to their depths because of him. Yea, so be it. Amen.

'I am the Alpha and the Omega,' says the Divine Lord,

'who is,
who was,
who will be,
who rules the universe.'

I, John, your brother who shares the trials and the kingship and the endurance to which Jesus calls us, was on the island called Patmos for the sake of the Word of God and the truth concerning Jesus. And there, on the Lord's day, the spiritual world was opened to me and I heard from behind me a powerful voice like a trumpet-call which said:

'Write down in a book what you see, and send it to the seven churches – to Ephesus, and Smyrna, and Pergamum, and Thyatira, and Sardes, and Philadelphia and Laodicea'.

So I turned round to see what voice it was that was speaking to me. And as I turned I saw seven golden candlesticks and in the midst of these candlesticks the figure of the Son of Man. He was clothed in a long robe down to his feet, and with a golden girdle around his breast. His head and his hair were white like snow-white wool, his eyes like flaming fire, his feet like white-hot brass melted in the furnace, and his voice like the sound of rushing waters. He held in his right hand seven stars, and a sharp double-edged sword came out of his mouth. His countenance was like the sun shining in full strength.

When I saw him, I fell at his feet like a dead man. But he, laying his right hand upon me said:

'Do not be afraid. I am the I am, who was at the beginning and shall be at the end, and who lives now. I passed through death, and see, I am alive through all cycles of time. And I hold the keys of death and of the land of the shades. Write down what you see, what is now, and what will occur hereafter. The secret meaning of the seven stars which you see in my right hand and of the seven golden candlesticks is this:

the seven stars are the angels of the seven churches, and the seven candlesticks are the seven churches themselves.

Chapters 2 and 3

'To the Angel of the Church at Ephesus write:
Thus speaks he who himself has power over the seven stars in his right hand and who walks amidst the seven golden lamps: I know your ways and your labour and your power to endure. I know also that you cannot bear with those who are evil. You have tested self-styled "Apostles", who are nothing of the kind, and have found them out to be liars.

'You have patience. For the sake of my name you have suffered and not grown weary. But I hold against you that you have left your first love. Think of the heights from which you have fallen. Turn and do as you did in the beginning, or I will come and remove your lamp from its place unless you change. But one thing you have, you hate the ways of the Nicolaitans, which I also hate.

'He who has ears to hear, let him hear what the Spirit says to the churches.

'To him who wins through I will give leave to eat from the tree of life, which stands in the paradise of God.

*   *   *

'And to the Angel of the Church at Smyrna write:
Thus speaks the first and the last, who passed through death and has come alive: I know your distress, and your poverty, though you are rich – and the cursing of those who pretend to be Jews but are a school of Satan. Have no fear of the suffering which is in store for you. See, the devil will throw some of you into prison in order that you may be tested. A time of distress lasting ten days awaits you. Be faithful unto death, and I will give you the crown of life.

'He who has ears, let him hear what the Spirit says to the churches.

'He who wins through shall not be hurt by the second death.

*   *   *

'And to the Angel of the Church at Pergamum write:
Thus speaks he who wields the sharp two-edged sword: I know where your home is – where the throne of Satan stands.

'You hold firmly to my name and have not denied your faith in me even in the days when Antipas, my faithful witness, was killed in your midst, in the very house of Satan.

'But there are a few things which I hold against you. You have some among your people who maintain the teaching of Balaam who taught Balak to ensnare the sons of Israel, to make them eat the flesh of pagan sacrifices and to share in orgiastic rites. And you, too, have some who similarly hold the teaching of the Nicolaitans.

'Change your ways, or else I will come to you quickly and make war upon them with the sword of my mouth.

'He who has ears, let him hear what the Spirit says to the churches.

'To him who wins through I will give of the secret food from heaven, and I will give him a white stone and a new name written on the stone which no one can tell but he who receives it.

*　　*　　*

'And to the Angel of the Church at Thyatira write:
Thus speaks the Son of God who has eyes like a flame of fire and whose feet are like white-hot brass: I know your ways, and your love and your faith and your service and your patience, and your latest works to be even greater than your first. But I hold against you that you allow the woman Jezebel, who calls herself a prophetess, to teach and to seduce my servants that they share in orgies and eat the flesh of pagan sacrifices. I have given her time to change her ways, but she does not wish to part with her fornication. See, I throw her into a sickbed and all those who have sinned with her into great distress, unless they repent of their ways.

'And I will destroy her children by death; then all the churches shall know that I am the I am who searches the living organs and the hearts, and I shall give to each one of you what is his due according to his deeds.

'But I speak also to you others in Thyatira who do not hold this teaching, who have not known what they call "the deep things of Satan". I will not put another burden on you. But hold firmly what you have until I come.

'He who wins through and holds my ways to the end, to him will I give a power transcending races and nations. He shall shepherd them, and his crook shall be of iron. Like earthen vessels they shall be broken. He shall have the same "I" which I have received from the Father, and I will give him the morning star.

'He who has ears, let him hear what the Spirit says to the churches.

* * *

'To the Angel of the Church at Sardes write:
Thus speaks he who holds the seven Spirits of God and the seven stars: I know your deeds. You have a name for being alive, but in fact you are dead. Wake up and strengthen what is still left, and what is at the point of death. I have not found any of your tasks completed in the sight of my God. Recall therefore how you have received and heard the message; cherish this and re-think all things. If you fail to wake up (to higher consciousness), I may have come like a thief and you may never know at what hour I have come upon you.

'Yet here and there in Sardes you have individuals who have not soiled their garments, and who shall walk on my path with me clothed in white, for they are worthy. He who wins through will be clothed in white, and I will not remove his name from the Book of Life, but I will call his name before my Father and his angels.

'He who has ears, let him hear what the Spirit says to the churches.

* * *

'And to the Angel of the Church at Philadelphia write:
Thus speaks the Holy One, the Real One, who holds the key of David, who opens and no one shuts, and who shuts and no one opens: I know your ways. See, I have opened a door before

your eyes which no one can close. Your power is yet small but you have cherished my word and not denied my name. Behold, I will see to it that some of the school of Satan, who call themselves Jews although they are not, but lie, behold, I will see to it that they come and prostrate themselves at your feet; they shall know that I have loved you. You have preserved the word of my patience, and so I will preserve you in the hour of the great trial which will come upon the whole world in order to test those who live on the earth. I come quickly. Hold firm what you have, that no one may take away your crown.

'Him who wins through I will make a pillar in the temple of my God, and he shall never leave it any more. And I will inscribe into him the name of my God and the name of the city of my God, the New Jerusalem which descends out of heaven from my God; and I will inscribe into him my new name.

'He who has ears, let him hear what the Spirit says to the churches.

*   *   *

'And to the Angel of the Church at Laodicea write:
Thus speaks the Amen who vindicates faith and truth; the wellspring of the creation of God: I know your ways; you are neither cold nor hot. If only you were cold or hot! Since you are tepid and neither hot nor cold, I will spit you out of my mouth. You say, "I am rich and have plenty and miss nothing", and you do not realise how wretched and miserable and poor and blind and naked you are. I advise you to buy of me gold purified in the fire that you may be rich, and white garments that you may be clothed and that the shame of your nakedness be not visible, and ointment to anoint your eyes that you may see.

'The I AM tests and trains those whom he loves. So kindle the fire of your heart and change your ways. Behold, I stand at the door and knock. If anyone hears my voice and opens the door I will go in to him and will share the meal with him, and he with me.

'He who wins through, to him will I grant to take his seat with me on my throne, even as I also have won through and have taken my seat with my Father on his throne.

163

'He who has ears, let him hear what the Spirit says to the churches.'

Chapter 4

After this, I looked and I saw that a door was open in heaven. And in my ears was the first voice which had spoken to me like a trumpet, and it said:

'Come up here, and I will show you what must occur in the future, after all that has gone before.'

And immediately I found myself in the realm of the spirit.

A throne stood there in heaven and one who sat on the throne. His appearance blazed like crystal-white jasper and rose cornelian. And a rainbow shining like an opalescent emerald encircled the throne. Around the throne twenty-four other thrones, and upon them twenty-four elders were seated, clothed in white robes, with golden crowns on their heads.

From the throne lightning flashes forth, and voices are heard and thunders roar.

And seven flaming torches are burning before the throne. These are the seven Creator-Spirits of God.

Before the throne it is like a sea of glass as clear as crystal. And up to half of the height of the throne and encircling it are four living beings full of eyes at the front and the back.

The first living being resembles a lion, the second a bull, the third has a face like a human being, and the fourth appears like an eagle in flight. These four living beings have six wings each. All over them and even within them they abound with eyes.

And without ceasing day and night they sing:

'Holy, holy, holy the Divine Lord,
who rules the universe,
who was,
who is,
who will be.'

And whenever those living beings offer glory, honour and thanksgiving to him who sits on the throne and who is the bearer of life through all cycles of time, the twenty-four elders bow down before him who sits on the throne and worship him who bears life through all cycles of time, and lay down their crowns before the throne and say:

'Our Lord and God, thou art worthy to assume the glory of life and the dignity of soul and the power of spirit. For thou didst create all things and by thy will they came into being and were created.'

Chapter 5

And I saw on the right hand of him who was seated on the throne a scroll covered with writing on both sides, inside and on the back, and sealed with seven seals. And I saw a mighty angel who called out with a loud voice: 'Who is worthy to open the scroll and to break its seals?'

And no one in heaven, or on earth, or under the earth was able to open the scroll or to look into it. And I began to weep bitterly because no one was found worthy to open the scroll or to look into it. Then one of the elders said to me:

'Do not weep. See, the Lion from the tribe of Judah, the Root of David, is victorious and able to open the scroll and to break its seven seals.'

Then I saw in the very centre of the throne and of the four living beings and in the midst of the elders a Lamb standing there as if it had been made a sacrifice. He had seven horns and seven eyes, and the seven eyes are the seven Creator-Spirits of God issuing into the whole earth. And he went and took the scroll from the right hand of him who was seated on the throne.

And when he took the scroll, the four living beings and the twenty-four elders fell down before the Lamb. Each of them had a harp and golden vessels overflowing with clouds of sweet incense. These are the prayers of the spirit-devoted souls. And they sing a new song, saying:

'Worthy art thou to take the scroll and to break its seals, for thou wast slain and thy blood hast purchased for God men from every tribe, and tongue, and nation, and race, and hast made them a kingdom and priests for our God, and they shall reign as kings upon the earth.'

And in my vision I heard the voice of many angels encircling the throne, the living beings and the elders. Their number was myriads of myriads and thousands of thousands, crying with a loud voice:

'Worthy is the Lamb who was slain to receive power, wealth and wisdom and the strength of spirit, the dignity of soul, the glory of life, and the power to bless.'

And then I heard the voice of every creature in heaven, and on earth, and under the earth and in the sea and all that are in them saying:

'The power to bless, the dignity of soul, and the glory of life and creative might belong to him who sits on the throne and to the Lamb through all cycles of time.'

And the four living beings said 'Amen', and the elders fell down and worshipped.

Chapter 6

And I saw the Lamb break the first of the seven seals. And I heard one of the living beings cry with a voice of thunder:
'Come forth!'
And I saw, and there appeared a white horse. Its rider carried a bow; and he was given a crown. He rode out victorious from victory to victory.
And when he broke the second seal, I heard the second living being cry:
'Come forth!'
And another horse came out, which was red. And its rider was given power to take away peace from the earth, so that men should kill each other. And he was given a great sword.
And when he broke the third seal, I heard the third living being cry:
'Come forth!'
And I saw, and there appeared a black horse. And its rider had a pair of scales in his hand. And I heard a voice which seemed to come from the midst of the living beings say:

'A measure of wheat for a shilling, and three measures of barley for a shilling – but do not tamper with the oil or the wine.'

And when he broke the fourth seal, I heard the voice of the fourth living being cry:

'Come forth!'

And I saw, and there appeared a deathly pale horse. And the name of its rider was Death, and the shades of the underworld followed him. And they were given over a quarter of the earth, to kill with the sword, and by famine, and the plague and the wild beasts of the earth.

And when he broke the fifth seal, I saw beneath the altar the souls of those who had been slain for the sake of the Word of God and because of their faithful testimony. And they cried with a loud voice, saying:

'How long will it be, O Master, holy and true, until thou wilt judge and avenge our blood upon those who live on the earth?'

Then each one of them was given a white garment, and they were told to wait in peace a little longer, until the whole number of their fellow-servants and of their brethren who were to die as they did should be made up.

And I saw him break the sixth seal. There was a tremendous earthquake. And the sun grew dark as if covered with sackcloth, and the full moon turned red like blood. And the stars of heaven fell to the earth, just as a fig tree drops its unripe figs when shaken by a gale. The sky vanished like a scroll rolled up, and every mountain and island was jolted out of its place.

And the kings of the earth, and the great men, and the captains, and the rich people, and the powerful, and every man, slave or free, hid themselves in the caves and among the rocks of the mountains. And they called out to the mountains and the rocks:

'Fall down upon us and hide us from the face of him who sits upon the throne and from the indignation of the Lamb. For the great day of their wrath has come, and who is able to stand up to it?'

167

After this I saw four angels standing at the four corners of the earth restraining the four winds of the earth, so that no wind should blow on the earth or on the sea or on any tree. And I saw another angel ascending out of the sunrise, carrying the seal of the God of Life. And he cried out with a mighty voice to the four angels to whom power was given to harm the earth and the sea:

'Do no harm to the earth, nor to the sea, nor to the trees, until we have sealed the servants of our God upon their foreheads.'

And I heard the number of those who were sealed; there were sealed 144,000, from every tribe of the sons of Israel:

From the tribe of Judah, twelve thousand,
From the tribe of Reuben, twelve thousand,
From the tribe of Gad, twelve thousand,
From the tribe of Asher, twelve thousand,
From the tribe of Naphtali, twelve thousand,
From the tribe of Manasseh, twelve thousand,
From the tribe of Simeon, twelve thousand,
From the tribe of Levi, twelve thousand,
From the tribe of Issachar, twelve thousand,
From the tribe of Zebulun, twelve thousand,
From the tribe of Joseph, twelve thousand,
From the tribe of Benjamin, twelve thousand.

After this I had another vision and saw a vast assembly, which no man could have numbered, from all races and tribes and nations and languages. They stood in the presence of the throne and in the presence of the Lamb, clothed in white robes, and with palm branches in their hands. And with a great shout they cry:

'Salvation belongs to our God who sits upon the throne, and to the Lamb.'

And all the angels stood in a circle round the throne and the elders and the four living beings, and they prostrated themselves before the throne and worshipped God and said:

'Amen! Benediction, glory, wisdom, selfgiving, dignity, potency and strength belong to our God through all cycles of time; Amen!'

Then one of the elders addressed me and said:
'Those who are clothed in white robes – who are they and where do they come from?'
I said to him, 'You know, my lord.'
And he said to me:
'These are the souls of those who have come through the great trial, and have washed their robes white in the blood of the Lamb. Therefore they are in the presence of the throne of God and serve him day and night in his temple. And he who is seated on the throne will shelter them. They will neither hunger nor thirst any more, nor will the sun beat upon them nor any scorching heat oppress them. For the Lamb who is raised to the throne will be their shepherd and will lead them to fountains from which there springs the water of life. And God will wipe away every tear from their eyes.'

Chapters 8 and 9

And when he broke the seventh seal, there was utter silence in heaven for what seemed like half an hour. And I saw the seven angels who stand before God, and they were given seven trumpets.

And the other angel came and stepped in front of the altar holding a golden censer. He was given a large amount of incense that he should add it to the prayers of all the spirit-devoted souls to be offered upon the golden altar before the throne. And the smoke of the incense rose up, together with the prayers of the saints, from the hand of the angel who stands before God. And the angel took the censer, filled it with fire f rom the altar, and hurled it upon the earth. And thunderings, voices, flashes of lightning and an earthquake followed.

Then the seven angels who held the seven trumpets prepared to blow them.

And the first angel blew his trumpet. And hail and fire, mingled with blood, formed itself and was hurled upon the earth. And a third part of the earth was burnt up, and one-third of all the trees was burnt up, and every blade of green grass was burnt up.

And the second angel blew his trumpet. And something like a great mountain blazing with fire was thrown into the sea. And a third part of the sea turned into blood, a third of the living creatures in the sea died, and a third of all ships was destroyed.

And the third angel blew his trumpet. And a huge star fell from the sky blazing like a torch, and it fell upon a third of the rivers and upon the fountains of water. The name of the star is called Absinthus (wormwood). And a third part of the waters turned into wormwood, and many people died because the waters had become so bitter.

And the fourth angel blew his trumpet. And a third part of the sun was smitten, and a third part of the moon, and a third part of the stars, so that a third part of their light was darkened, and did not shine, neither by day nor by night.

Then I saw a solitary eagle flying in mid-heaven, and I heard him cry aloud:

'Woe, woe, woe to the inhabitants of the earth because of the remaining trumpet blasts of the three angels who are yet to blow their trumpets.'

And the fifth angel blew his trumpet. And I saw a star that had fallen down from heaven to the earth, and he was given the key of the bottomless pit. And smoke like the smoke of a great furnace rose out of the pit, and the light of the sun and the air grew dark from the smoke of the pit.

And out of the smoke locusts emerged to descend upon the earth. And they were given powers like the powers of earthly scorpions. They were told not to harm any grass, or any green thing, or any tree upon the earth, but to hurt only those human beings who did not bear the seal of God upon their foreheads. And they were charged not to kill men, but only to torture them for five months. And the torture which they could inflict was like the pain of a scorpion's sting. And in those days men will seek death but will not find it; and they will long to die, but death will elude them.

The shapes of the locusts appeared like horses prepared for battle. On their heads were what appeared to be crowns like gold, and their faces were like human faces, and they had hair like the hair of women. And their teeth were like the teeth of lions, and their breastplates were like iron breastplates, and the rattling of their wings was like the rattling of massed chariots charging into battle. And they have tails like scorpions, and stings, and it is in their tails that they have power to hurt men for five months.

They have as a king over them the angel of the pit, whose name in Hebrew is Abaddon, which is translated into Greek as Apollyon, (that is to say, he who destroys).

The first woe is past, but see, two more woes are coming after this.

And the sixth angel blew his trumpet. And I heard a solitary voice speaking from the four corners of the golden altar which stands before God. And it said to the sixth angel who held the trumpet:

'Release the four angels who are bound at the great river Euphrates.'

And the four angels were released, who had been held ready for the hour, the day, the month and the year, to kill one-third of mankind. And the number of the army of horsemen was two hundred thousand thousand – I heard what their number was. And thus I saw the horses in the vision and their riders: they had breastplates of fiery red, hyacinth blue and sulphurous colour. And the heads of the horses looked like lions, and out of their mouths poured fire and smoke and sulphur. A third of mankind died from these three evil things: the fire, the smoke and the sulphur which pour out of their mouths. For the power of these horses lies in their mouths and in their tails. Indeed, their tails are like serpents with heads, and with them they do harm.

But the rest of mankind who were not killed by these plagues did not repent of their ways and of their doings, nor ceased to worship evil spirits and idols of gold, silver, brass, stone or wood, which can neither see nor hear nor walk. Neither did they repent of their murders, of their sorceries, or their orgies or their thieving.

And I saw another powerful angel descending from heaven. He was clothed in a cloud, and the rainbow shone around his head. His countenance blazed like the sun, and his legs were like pillars of fire. He held a tiny book open in his hand. He planted his right foot upon the sea and his left foot upon the land and called out with a loud voice like the roar of a lion. And when he had called, the seven thunders raised their voices. And when the seven thunders had raised their voices, I was about to write. And I heard a voice out of the heavenly spheres saying:

'Seal up what the seven thunders said; do not write it down.'

Then the angel whom I saw standing upon the sea and upon the land lifted his right hand up to heaven and solemnly declared by him who lives through all cycles of time, who created the heavens and all that is therein, and the earth and all that is therein, and the sea and all that is therein:

'There shall be no more time.* But in the days of the trumpet blast of the seventh angel, when he begins to blow, the hidden mysteries of God will be made complete, as he foretold it to his servants the prophets.'

And the voice which I had heard from heaven spoke to me again and said:

'Go and take the tiny book which lies open in the hand of the angel who bestrides the sea and the land.'

And I went towards the angel, asking him to give me the tiny book. And he said to me:

'Take it and eat it up. It will be bitter to your stomach, but sweet as honey in your mouth.'

And I took the tiny book from the hand of the angel, and swallowed it. And it was in my mouth as sweet as honey, but when I had eaten it up, my stomach became bitter.

Then they said to me: 'You must prophesy anew about many nations and races and tongues and kings.'

And I was given a reed like a staff and I was told, 'Rise up

* 'Time shall no longer continue'; 'There shall be no more space-time'; 'Regular time has run out (shall now cease)' are alternative renderings of this sentence shown in Alfred Heidenreich's MS.

and take the measure of the temple of God and of the altar and of those who worship there. But leave out the courtyard outside the temple. Do not take its measure at all, for it has been given over to the heathen races, who will walk in the holy city for forty-two months.

'And I will charge my two witnesses clothed in sackcloth that they should proclaim the spirit-word for 1,260 days.'

These are the two olive trees and the two candlesticks which stand before the Lord of the earth. If anyone wants to hurt them, fire issues from their mouths and consumes their enemies. Indeed, if anyone wants to hurt them, this is the manner in which he must die. These witnesses have power to shut up the sky so that no rain may fall during the days of their prophetic service. They have also power over the waters and can turn them into blood and can strike the earth with any plague as often as they wish.

And when they have fulfilled their prophetic service, the animal which comes up from the pit will go to war against them. It will defeat them and kill them. And their dead bodies will lie in the street of the great city, which is called by its occult name, Sodom and Egypt. There also their Lord was crucified.

Men from all nations and tribes and tongues and races shall gaze upon their dead bodies for three and a half days, and will not allow their bodies to be buried. And the inhabitants of the earth will gloat over them and rejoice and send one another presents because these two prophets had tried them sorely.

But after three and a half days, the life-giving Spirit from God entered into them, and they stood up on their feet. This struck terror into the hearts of those who were watching them and they heard a tremendous voice calling from heaven to these two: 'Come up here!' And they rose up to heaven in a cloud, and their enemies saw them.

At the same moment there was a great earthquake, and the tenth part of the city fell in ruins, and seven thousand people were killed in the earthquake. The rest were terrified and acknowledged the glory of the God of Heaven.

The second woe is past. See, the third woe comes quickly.

173

And the seventh angel blew his trumpet. There arose loud voices in heaven saying:

'The world has become the kingdom of our Lord and of his Christ, and he will be king through all cycles of time.'

Then the twenty-four elders who sit on their thrones in the presence of God fell on their faces and worshipped God saying:

'We thank thee O Lord,
who art God and ruler of all,
who is,
and who was,
that thou hast assumed thy great power and hast begun to reign. The races of the world were full of fury, but now the fierce passion of thy will has come. The season is at hand when the fate of the dead is decided, and justice is done to thy servants the prophets and the souls devoted to the spirit and to all who stand in awe of thy name, both small and great, and now is the time to destroy the destroyers of the earth.'

Then the temple of God in the heavenly spheres was thrown open, and the Ark of his Covenant became visible within his temple. And lightnings flashed, and voices were heard, and thunders roared and the earth quaked and a great hail storm broke.

Chapter 12

Then a great portent became visible in the heavenly spheres: a woman clothed with the sun, with the moon under her feet, and a crown of twelve stars upon her head. Being pregnant, she cried out in her labour and in the pains of giving birth to her child.

Then another portent became visible in the heavenly spheres. I saw a huge fiery-red dragon with seven heads and ten horns, and with a diadem on each of his heads. His tail dragged down a third of the stars in heaven, and flung them to the earth. And the dragon stood facing the woman who was about to give birth, intent to devour her child as soon as it was born. And she gave birth to the son who is to shepherd all nations with a crook of iron.

And her child was snatched away by God to his throne. And the woman fled into the desert where God had predestined that she should stay and be sustained for one thousand, two hundred and sixty days.

Then war broke out in heaven. Michael and his angels opened the fight against the dragon. And the dragon and his angels fought back. But their strength failed them and there was no longer any place for them in heaven. So the great dragon was overthrown, the primeval serpent who is known as Devil and as Satan, who would wreck the whole world. He was hurled down to the earth, and his angels were hurled down with him.

And I heard a great voice in heaven cry:

'Now the healing and the might and the kingdom of our God and the creative power of his Christ have come into their own. For the accuser of our brethren has been overthrown, who said evil things against them before our God day and night. They have defeated him through the blood of the Lamb, and through the Word of their witness; they did not hold their lives so dear as to fear death. Therefore rejoice, O heavenly spheres, and all you who live in them. But woe for the earth and the sea, for the Devil has come down to you in a great passion, knowing that his time will be short.'

And when the dragon saw that he had been thrown down upon the earth, he began to pursue the woman who had given birth to the Male Being. But the woman was given the two wings of the great eagle, so that she could fly to her place in the desert, where she is provided for, away from the serpent, for a time and times and half a time. Then the serpent ejected water from his mouth and it rushed like a river after the woman to carry her away by its flood. But the earth came to the rescue of the woman; it opened its mouth and drank up the river which the dragon had emitted from his mouth. Then the dragon was filled with fury against the woman and went away to make war upon those who remain of her offspring. They are those who cherish the purposes of God and hold fast to the testimony of Jesus.

Chapter 13

Then I stood on the sandy shore of the ocean and I saw an animal rise up from the sea, with seven heads and ten horns. There were ten diadems on its horns and blasphemous titles upon its heads. This animal which I saw looked like a leopard, although it had feet like a bear and a mouth like the mouth of a lion.

And the dragon gave it his own strength and his throne and full power and authority. One of its heads showed something that looked like a deadly wound of sacrifice, but this had been healed.

And the whole earth admired the animal and followed it; and they adored the dragon because he had given power and authority to the animal. And they worshipped the animal, too, saying: 'Who is like the animal? And who can defy it?'

And its mouth was allowed to speak monstrous things and blasphemies; and it was given freedom to do its work for forty-two months.

And it opened its mouth in blasphemies against God, blaspheming his name, and his dwelling place, and those who dwell in the heavenly spheres.

And it was permitted to make war upon the saints and to defeat them, and its sway extended over every tribe and nation and language and race. And all the souls living on earth will worship it, all those whose names have not been written in the Book of Life, which belongs to the Lamb whose sacrifice is the foundation of the world.

He that has an ear, let him hear:
He who puts others in prison
into prison he will go.
He who kills with the sword
with the sword he must be killed.

Here is shown the patient endurance and the faith of the saints.

And I saw another animal rise out of the earth; it had two horns like a ram, but spoke with the voice of a dragon. It exerts the full power and authority of the first animal on its behalf. And it makes the earth and all who live on it worship the first animal, the one with the mortal wound which had been healed.

It performs works of magic; it makes fire fall from heaven to earth before men's eyes. It leads astray those who live on the earth by the magic which it is empowered to work on behalf of and in the sight of the animal, and it tells the people on earth to erect an image in honour of the animal which received the sword-wound but stayed alive. And it was allowed to pour breath of life into the image of the animal so that the image of the animal could speak and cause all those to be put to death who refuse to worship the image of the animal.

And it forces all, small and great, rich and poor, free men and slaves, to receive a mark on their right hand or on their forehead, with the intention that no one should be able to buy or sell unless he bears the mark, the name of the animal or the numerical value of its name.

Let wisdom speak here: those with thinking minds should seek the meaning of the number of the animal. For it is the number of man; and its number is six hundred and sixty-six.

Chapter 14

Then I had a further vision. I saw the Lamb standing on Mount Sion, and with him one hundred and forty-four thousand who had his name and the name of his father written upon their foreheads.

And I heard a sound coming from heaven like the roar of rushing waters and the roll of heavy thunder. Yet I heard it like the music of harpers harping with their harps. They sing a song of renewal before the throne and before the four living beings and before the elders. No one could learn that song except the one hundred and forty-four thousand who were redeemed from the bonds of the earth.

These are souls who have not gone after idols through the instincts of the blood, for they have kept the integrity of their spirit. They follow the path of the Lamb wherever he leads. They are redeemed as the beginning of a new humanity, under God and the Lamb. No falsehood has come from their lips. They are untainted.

And I saw another angel flying in mid-heaven, bearing the everlasting gospel to proclaim it to all mankind on the earth, to every race and tribe and language and nation.

He cried with a loud voice:

'Now stand in awe before God and acknowledge his glory. For the hour of his judgement and decision is come. Worship him who made heaven and earth, the sea and the springs of water.'

And another, a second angel, followed crying:

'Fallen, fallen is Babylon the great! She who made all races drink of the wine of her passionate idolatry.'

And another, a third angel, followed these two crying in a loud voice:

'If any man worships the animal and its image and receives its mark upon his forehead or his hand, he shall drink of the wine of God's passion, poured undiluted into the cup of his wrath. He must stand the test of purification by fire and purging sulphur before the holy angels and before the Lamb. And the smoke of the fire of their purification rises up through the timeless ages; there is no respite from it day or night. Such is the fate of those who worship the animal and its image, and who accept the mark of its name.'

Here the endurance of the saints stands out who cherish the purposes of God and keep their trust in Jesus.

And I heard a voice from heaven say:

'Write! Blessed are the dead who die in the Lord, henceforth.'

'Yea,' says the Spirit, 'they may rest their bruises for their deeds do go with them.'

Then I had a further vision and I saw a white cloud and sitting upon the cloud the likeness of the Son of Man, with a golden crown on his head and a sharp sickle in his hand. And again an angel came out of the temple, calling in a loud voice to him who sat on the cloud:

'Thrust in your sickle, and reap; for the hour of reaping has come, and the harvest of the earth is ripe.'

Then he who sat on the cloud swung his sickle upon the earth, and the reaping of the earth was done.

And once more an angel came out of the temple in heaven, and he also had a sharp sickle. And from the altar another angel came out who is in charge of the fire. He called in a loud voice to the angel with the sickle:

'Thrust in your sickle and harvest the clusters of the vine of the earth, for the grapes are fully ripe.'

Then the angel swung his sickle upon the earth, and gathered the harvest of the vine of the earth, and threw it into the great winepress of the impassioned will of God. And the winepress was trodden outside the city, and out of the winepress a stream of blood, as high as the horses' bridles, flowed for a distance of two hundred miles.

Chapter 15

Then I saw another portentous image in heaven, great and awe-inspiring; seven angels holding in store the seven last trials – the last ones, for in them the creative passion of God is consummated.*

And I saw what appeared like a sea of glass shot through with fire, and standing upon that sea of glass I saw those who had come out victorious from the struggle with the animal, its image, and the being which is signified by its number. They held harps from God in their hands. And they sing the song of Moses, the servant of God, and the song of the Lamb, saying:

'Great and awe-inspiring are thy deeds, O divine Lord and ruler of all. Thy ways lead to goodness and truth, O king of the nations. Who would not stand in awe before thee, O Lord, and acknowledge the glory of thy being? For thou alone art holy. All people of the earth shall come and worship

* Alternatively – the consuming love of God achieves its final purpose.

before thee, for thy creative judgements (resolutions) have become manifest.'

And after this I saw the temple opened in heaven, the tabernacle of affirmation, and out of the temple came the seven angels who hold the seven plagues. They were clothed in spotless shining linen, and they were girded round their breasts with golden girdles.

And one of the four living creatures gave to the seven angels seven golden bowls heavy with the impassioned will of God who is the bearer of life through all cycles of time. And the temple was filled with the shining vapour of glory and power which came from God. And no one could enter the temple until the seven plagues of the seven angels were consummated.

Chapter 16

And I heard a mighty voice from the temple saying to the seven angels:

'Go and pour out upon the earth the seven bowls of God's consuming passion.'

And the first one went and emptied his bowl upon the earth. And loathsome and malignant ulcers befell all those men who bore the mark of the animal and who worshipped its image.

And the second angel emptied his bowl into the sea which turned into liquid like the decomposed blood of a corpse, and every living thing in the sea died.

And the third angel emptied his bowl into the rivers and fountains of water and they turned into blood. And I heard the angel of the waters say:

'Just art thou, who art and who hast been, thou holy one, in these thy judgements. For they have shed the blood of the saints and prophets, and now thou hast given them blood to drink. This is what they deserve.'

And I heard the altar say:

'Yea, O divine Lord, ruler of all, thy judgements are true and right.'

And the fourth angel emptied his bowl over the sun. And the sun was given power to burn men with fiery heat. Then men were scorched by terrible heat, so that they screamed curses against the name of God who has power over these afflictions; but they closed their minds to the revelation of God and to any change of their ways.

And the fifth angel emptied his bowl upon the throne of the animal. Its kingdom was plunged into darkness. Men gnawed their tongues in pain, and cursed the God of heaven because of their pain and their ulcers, but refused to change their mind or their ways.

And the sixth angel emptied his bowl upon the great river Euphrates. And its waters dried up so that the way for the kings of the east might be prepared.

Then I saw three foul spirits, looking like frogs, come out of the mouth of the dragon, the animal and the false prophet. They are diabolical spirits which work magic upon the kings of the whole earth to bring them together to battle on the great day of God, the ruler of all.

'See, I come like a thief! Blessed is he who stays awake and keeps his clothes ready, so that he will not have to walk naked and men see his deformity.'

And they led them together to the place called in Hebrew, Armageddon.

And the seventh angel emptied his bowl into the air. And a mighty voice came out of the temple from the throne saying:

'This is the end.'

And lightning flashed and voices were heard and thunders roared, and a tremendous tremor shook the earth, the like of which had never happened since mankind lived on the earth; so tremendous was this earthquake.

And the great city was divided into three parts, and the cities of the nations fell in ruins. And God called to mind Babylon the great and made her drink the cup of the wine of his impassioned wrath. Every island fled and the mountains vanished. And big hailstones like hundredweights fell from heaven upon men; and men cursed God for the blows of the hail, for it beat upon them with savage blows.

Chapter 17

Then came one of the seven angels who held the seven bowls and talked to me. 'Come,' he said, 'I will show you the doom of the great harlot who is seated upon many waters, and with her the kings of the earth have practised apostacy and those who live on the earth have become drunk with the wine of her perversion.'

And he led me in the spirit into a desert place. And I saw the woman upon a scarlet animal covered with blasphemous titles and having seven heads and ten horns. The woman was dressed in purple and scarlet, ornate with gold, jewels and pearls. In her hand she held a golden cup full of ghastly idols and filthy creations of her indecency. On her forehead a name is written, an occult phrase, *Babylon the great, mother of harlots and the abominations of the earth.*

And I saw that the woman was drunk with the blood of the saints and of those who bore witness to Jesus. And as I watched her I was filled with utter astonishment.

But the angel said to me, 'Why are you so astonished? I am here to tell you the occult significance of the woman and of the animal with the seven heads and ten horns which carries her. The animal which you see has had its time, but has it no more; it will rise up from the pit only to meet its destruction. And those on the earth whose name is not written in the Book of Life since the foundation of the world will be astonished when they see the animal, which once was, and is not, and yet will appear.

'This needs a mind with higher knowledge. As for the seven heads, they are seven mountains on which the woman takes her seat. They are at the same time seven kings; five of them have been dethroned, one is here now, and the other has not yet come, and when he comes, he must remain only for a short time.

'And the animal which has had its time but no longer has now, is an eighth king which belongs to the seven, but it only goes to destruction.

'And the ten horns which you saw are ten kings who have not yet assumed their reign but they will receive power as kings for one hour together with the animal. They are of one mind and will put their strength and authority at the disposal of the animal. They will go to war with the Lamb and the Lamb will conquer them, for he is Lord of lords and King of kings, and with him are those who are called and chosen and faithful.'

And he said to me: 'The waters which you saw on which the harlot took her seat are nations and masses and races and languages. And the ten horns which you saw and the animal will loathe the harlot and will leave her deserted and stripped. They will devour her flesh and burn her with fire. For God has put into their hearts to carry out his purpose (resolution), and to be of one mind and to hand over their kingship to the animal, until such time that the words of God have achieved their goal.

'The woman whom you saw is the great city which dominates the kings of the earth.'

Chapter 18

After this I saw another angel coming down from heaven, endowed with great power and authority, and the very earth shone with the splendour of his being. His voice rang out and he cried:

'Fallen, fallen is Babylon the great! She has become a haunt of demons, and a prison of every foul spirit, and a cage of every ominous and hateful bird. For all the nations have drunk of the wine of her passionate apostacy, and the kings of the earth have practised idolatry with her, and the merchants of the earth have grown rich from the recklessness of her dissipation.'

And I heard another voice from heaven say:

'Come out of her, O my people, lest you be drawn into the community of her sins and must share the blows of her fate. For her sins have mounted up to the heavens, and God has called to mind the record of her wickedness. Give her back what she has given you; give her back double for what she has done. In the cup which she mixed for others, mix her a drink of twice the strength. For her self-glorification and her self-indulgence, give her purging torture and grief in equal measure. For she says in her heart, "Here I am seated a queen; I am no lonely widow and I shall never know sorrow." Therefore in a single day her fate shall strike her – death, grief and famine, and she shall be burned in the fire. For stern and strong is the Lord who passes divine judgement on her.'

And the kings of the earth who indulged with her in idolatry and wild extravagance will wail and beat their breasts over her when they see the smoke of her burning. Standing far off, terrified by her fateful trial, they cry:

'Alas, alas for the great city, for Babylon the mighty city, that in one single hour the crisis should come upon you!'

And the merchants of the earth shall also wail and grieve over her, for there is no one left to buy their goods – cargoes of gold and silver and jewels and pearls, and fine linen and purple and silk and scarlet, and all kinds of scented wood, and every kind of ivory vessel, every kind of vessel of most precious wood, of brass, iron and marble; cinnamon, spice, incense, myrrh, resin of frankincense, wine, oil, fine flour and corn; cattle and sheep, horses and chariots, and the bodies and souls of men.

'The fruit of your harvest which your heart desired is gone from you for ever; all your finery and brilliance are lost to you and none of it will be found any more.'

The merchants of those goods who have grown wealthy from her will stand far off, terrified by her fateful trial, weeping and lamenting, and saying:

'Alas, alas for the great city that was dressed in fine linen, and purple and scarlet, and covered with gold, jewels and pearls! For in one single hour all this great wealth was turned into wasteland.'

And every shipmaster and crew, all sailors and others whose business is upon the sea, stood far off and cried out when they saw the smoke of her burning:

'What city was ever like the great city?'

And they threw dust upon their heads, weeping and lamenting and cried:

'Alas, alas for the great city where all who had ships on the sea grew rich from her treasure. For in one single hour she is laid waste.'

('Rejoice over her fate, O heavenly spheres, with all the

184

saints, apostles and prophets! For God himself has pronounced judgement for you against her.')

And that one mighty angel lifted up a stone like a great millstone and threw it into the sea saying:

'Thus with a mighty sweep shall Babylon, the great city, be flung down, and shall never more be found. Never again shall the sound of harpists or musicians or flute-players or trumpeters be heard in you. Never again shall craftsmen of any craft be found in you, nor the sound of the grinding of the millstone be heard in you. No light of lamp shall ever shine in you again, nor the voice of the bridegroom or the bride be heard in you any more.

'Indeed your merchants were the great ones of the earth, and all the nations of the earth were thrown off their course by the spell of your magic.'

The blood of prophets and saints was discovered in her and the blood of all others ever shed on the earth in sacrifice.

Chapter 19

After this I heard what sounded like the mighty shout of a large crowd in heaven crying:

'Alleluia! Healing and Revelation and Power are the attributes of our God. His decisions lead to truth and goodness. He has passed judgement on the great harlot who corrupted the earth with her wickedness, and he has avenged the blood of his servants shed by her hand.'

And they cried a second time:

'Alleluia! The smoke of her destruction will not cease to rise up from this aeon to the next.'

Then the twenty-four elders and the four living creatures fell down and worshipped God who is seated upon the throne, saying:

'Amen. Alleluia!'

Then out of the throne a voice came, saying:

'Praise our God, all you who serve and revere him, both small and great!'

And I heard a noise like the voices of a large crowd and like the sound of rushing waters and the rolling of loud thunder saying:

'Alleluia! For the Lord our God, the ruler of all, has come into his kingdom. Let us be glad and rejoice, and praise his glorious revelation. For the wedding day of the Lamb has come, his bride has made herself ready. A dress of gleaming and spotless linen has been bestowed upon her. Such linen is the righteous fruit of souls devoted to the spirit.'

And he said to me: 'Write: Blessed are those who are called to the divine wedding banquet of the Lamb.' And he who spoke to me added: 'These are true words of God.'

And I fell at his feet to worship him, but he said to me:

'Do not do this. I am your fellow-servant and the fellow-servant of your brethren who have received the witness of Jesus. It is God whom you must worship.'

In this witness of Jesus lies the spiritual source of these prophecies.

Then I saw heaven wide open, and, lo, there was a white horse, and he who sat on it will make faith and knowledge true. His judgement and his fight are just. His eyes were like a flame of fire, and he had many diadems on his head. Written upon him was a name which no one knew but himself. And he had a robe wrapped around him which was dipped in blood. And the name which he was called was the Word of God.

And the armies in heaven followed him on white horses, clothed in linen white and pure. From his mouth there comes a sharp sword with which to strike the nations. He will shepherd mankind with an iron staff, and tread the winepress of the impassioned love of the almighty Being of God, the Ground of the World. And on his cloak and on his thigh he carries the name which is written: King of kings and Lord of lords.

And I saw that one angel stand in the sun; his voice rang out and he called to all the birds flying in mid-heaven:

'Come, flock together for the great meal which God

provides. Let your food be the flesh of the kings and the flesh of the captains, the flesh of strong men, the flesh of horses and their riders, the flesh of all men, free and unfree, small and great.'

And I saw the animal and the kings of the earth and their armies massed together for battle against the rider and his army. And the animal was taken prisoner and with it the false prophet who had worked magic in his presence, with which he had led astray those who accepted the mark of the animal and worshipped his image. They were thrown alive into the lake of fire which burns with purifying sulphur. The rest were killed by the sword which issues from the mouth of the rider upon the horse. And all the birds gorged themselves on their flesh.

Chapter 20

And I saw an angel descend from heaven who had the key of the pit and a large chain in his right hand. And he took hold of the dragon, the ancient serpent, in whom Devil and Satan are united, and bound him for a thousand years, and threw him into the pit, and locked and sealed it over him that he should no longer lead the nations astray until the thousand years are past. Then he must be let free for a short while.

And I saw thrones and those who were given the power to judge taking their seats on them.

And I saw the souls who were done to death because of their witness for Jesus and the Word of God, and those who had not worshipped the animal nor its image and who refused the sign of the animal on their forehead and on their hand. They came to life and reigned with Christ a thousand years. The rest of the dead did not come to life till the thousand years were past. This is the first resurrection. Blessed and exalted is he who shares in the first resurrection. Over such, the second death has no power. But they are priests of God and the Christ, and will reign with him for a thousand years.

And when the thousand years are completed, Satan will be set free from his prison, and he will go and lead astray the nations in all the four corners of the earth, Gog and Magog, and gather them for battle, whose number is like the sand of the sea shore.

They came up and spread over the breadth of the earth and encircled the army of the saints and the beloved city.

Then fire fell from heaven and devoured them. And the Devil who deceived them was thrown into the lake of fire and sulphur, to join the animal and the false prophet, and there they suffer pain day and night through the cycles of time.

And I saw a great shining throne and him who sat on it, before whose countenance the earth and the heaven fled and vanished.

And I saw the dead, both great and small, standing before the throne, and books were opened. And one book in particular was opened, the Book of Life. And the dead met their destiny according to their deeds on the basis of what was written in the book.

And the sea yielded its dead, and death and the land of shades yielded their dead, and everyone met his destiny according to his deeds. And death and the land of the shades were thrown into the lake of fire. And anyone who was not found written in the Book of Life was thrown into the lake of fire.

Chapter 21

And I saw a new heaven and a new earth. The former heaven and the former earth had passed away and the sea was no more. And I saw the Holy City, the New Jerusalem, descend from God out of the spiritual world, as beautiful as a bride prepared for her husband. And I heard a loud voice speak from the throne:

'Behold, God has pitched his tent among men. He will live among them, and they will be his people, and God in his very self will be with them. He will wipe away every tear from their eyes. Death will be no more, neither will there be sorrow or crying or pain. For all the former things are past.'

And he who is seated upon the throne said:
'See, I make all things new.'* And he added: 'Write, for these words are reliable and true.'

* Alternatively – I am creating a new universe.

And he said to me:

'It is done. I am Alpha and Omega, the Beginning and the End. I will give water from the Fountain of Life as my free gift to the thirsty. He who wins through will share in all these things, and I will be God to him and he will be son to me. But as for the cowards, the faithless and corrupt, the murderers and those who are wedded to matter, the addicts of magic, the worshippers of idols and all liars – their share is in the lake which burns with fire and sulphur, which is the second death.'

Then one of the seven angels who hold the seven bowls filled with the seven last blows of fate came to me and talked to me and said: 'Come; I will show you the Bride, the wife of the Lamb.'

And he carried me away in the spirit to the top of a great and high mountain and showed me the Holy City, Jerusalem, descending from God out of the spiritual world, radiant with the glory of God.

Her starlike brilliance sparkled like a most precious jewel, translucent like a crystal of jasper. She was surrounded by a great and lofty wall which had twelve gateways with twelve angels at the gates. There were twelve names inscribed which are the names of the twelve tribes of the sons of Israel.

On the east three gates, on the north three gates, on the south three gates and on the west three gates. The wall of the city has twelve foundation stones, and on these were engraved the twelve names of the twelve apostles of the Lamb.

And he who was talking to me had a golden measuring rod with which to measure the city and its gates and its wall. The city lies foursquare, its length equal to its breadth. And he measured the city with the rod, and it was twelve thousand furlongs, and the length and the breadth and the height of it are equal.

And he measured its wall. It is one hundred and forty-four cubits. This is the measure of the human being which is also the measure of the angel.

And the wall was built of jasper, and the city of purest gold, translucent like glass. The foundation stones of the wall of the city were adorned with every kind of precious stone. The first foundation stone was jasper, the second sapphire, the third agate, the fourth emerald, the fifth onyx, the sixth cornelian, the seventh chrysolyte, the eighth beryl, the ninth topaz, the tenth chrysoprasus, the eleventh hyacinth, the twelfth amethyst. The twelve gates were twelve pearls, each gate made of a single pearl. The street of the city was of purest gold, translucent through and through like glass.

A temple I did not see in the city. For the Lord, God, the ruler of all, himself is the temple, and the Lamb. The city has no need of the light of the sun or the moon, for the glory of God's revelation enlightens it and the Lamb is its lamp. The nations will walk by its light and the kings of the earth will bring their splendour into it.

The gates of the city will never be closed on any day, for there is no more nightfall. All that the nations hold glorious and honourable they will bring into it.

Nothing common shall ever enter into it, nor anyone doing false or base things, only those whose names are written in the Lamb's Book of Life.

Chapter 22

And he showed me the river of the Water of Life, clear as crystal, as it flowed from the throne of God and of the Lamb. In the middle of the street of the city and on either bank of the river grew the Tree of Life, bearing twelve kinds of fruit, a different one for each month. And the leaves of the tree were a healing medicine for the nations; and every curse has come to an end.

The throne of God and of the Lamb shall be within the city, and his servants shall celebrate his service. They shall see his face and his name will be upon their foreheads. Night shall be no more; they will no longer need the light of a candle or the light of the sun, for the Lord, God, will shed his light upon them, and they will reign as kings for all cycles of time.

Then he said to me:

'These are words of faith and truth. The Lord, God, who inspired the prophets, has sent his angel to show his servants what must swiftly come to pass.'

'See! I come quickly. Blessed is he who cherishes the prophetic words of this book.'

It is I, John, who have heard and seen these things. And when I heard and saw them I fell down to worship at the feet of the angel who showed them to me. But he said to me:

'No, do not do this. I am a fellow-servant to you and to your brother-prophets and to those who keep the words of this book. It is God whom you must worship.'

And he said to me:

'Do not seal up the prophetic words of this book. For the time has come.

'Who is wicked now shall remain wicked, and the sordid shall remain sordid. But the good man shall continue in his good deeds and he who is dedicated to the spirit shall remain so dedicated.'

'See, I come swiftly; and the return of each man's deeds which I am sharing out is coming with me. I am Alpha and Omega, the First and the Last, the origin and the fulfilment. Blessed are those who wash their robes, that they may have the right to the Tree of Life, and may enter through the gates into the city. But banned from the city are those who practise depraved rites, addicts of magic, those wedded to matter, the killers, demon-worshippers, and all lovers and practitioners of falsehood.

'I, Jesus, have sent my angel to you with this testimony for the Churches. I am the root and offspring of David, the bright morning star.'

And the Spirit and the Bride say, 'Come!'
And let everyone that hears say, 'Come!'
And let everyone who is still thirsty come. And let him who will take from the Water of Life as a free gift.
Now I solemnly declare to every man who hears the prophetic words of this book:

If anyone makes additions to these words, God will increase for him the calamities described in this book; and if anyone lessens the words of this prophetic book, God will take away from him his share in the Tree of Life and in the Holy City which are described in this book.

He who confirms these words says:

'Yes, I come swiftly!'
'Amen, come, Lord Jesus!'

The grace of the Lord Jesus be with all.